DICTATORS
in Cartoons

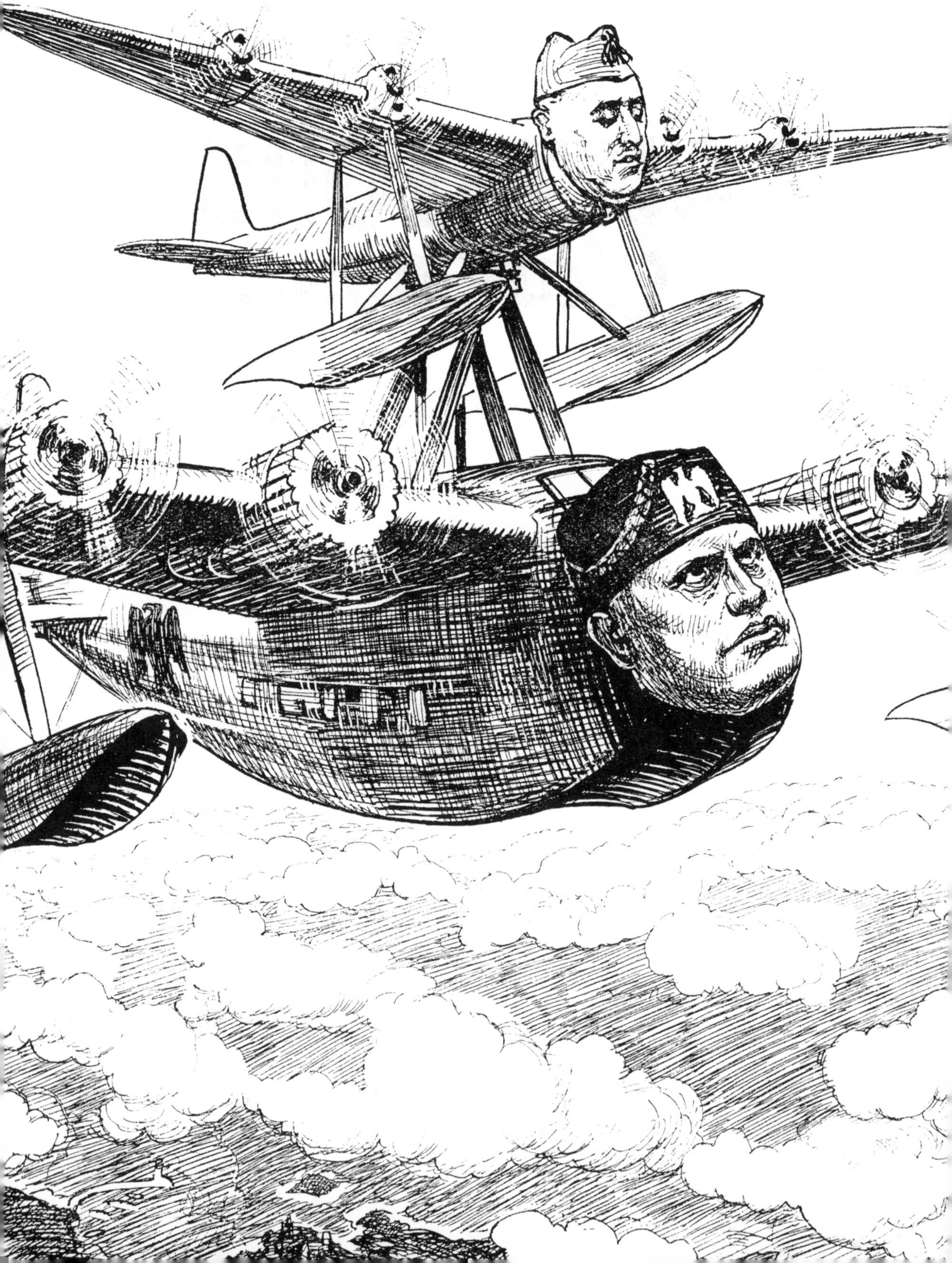

DICTATORS
in Cartoons

EDITED BY **TONY HUSBAND**

ARCTURUS

Designer: Zoe Mellors
Inhouse editor: Nigel Matheson

This edition published in 2015 by Arcturus Publishing Limited
26/27 Bickels Yard, 151–153 Bermondsey Street,
London SE1 3HA

ISBN: 978-1-78404-614-9
AD004475US

Printed in Malaysia

Contents

INTRODUCTION

Oh, to have been a fly on the wall when Hitler first clapped eyes on David Low's cartoons depicting him as a bumbling imbecile. Or imagine Mussolini flicking through the foreign papers and spluttering over his morning espresso at the E. H. Shepard cartoon showing him as a scarecrow that couldn't say boo to a goose.

It's doubtful whether the first impulse of a dictator is ever to laugh at himself. It's just not part of the job description. His preference is for the big gesture: wiping out rivals, crushing mutinies with big jackboots, and torturing and killing anyone who stands in his way. He likes to play nasty, and then wonders why people don't like him.

Above all, dictators seem to have a strong need to be admired. Most of us are happy to lead modest lives, but dictators are constantly trying to attract attention with rows of shiny medals, convoys of limos, and big, shouty speeches. They love nothing better than being applauded wherever they go.

But the price you pay for being a dictator is that people are always trying to knock you off your perch—especially cartoonists… As Aristotle and Plato pointed out long ago, laughter can break a despot's spell, undermine authority and lead to the overthrow of the state. As a tyrant, you instinctively know your days are numbered when people begin openly mocking you in the streets.

In this book, you'll find dictators and wielders of power transformed into midgets, hotel porters, moustachioed horses, even a humble pear. King Louis-Philippe of France hated being drawn as a pear so much that he eventually put the artist, Honoré Daumier, behind bars. But too late! The pear had become the symbol of his corrupt regime and anti-royalists were drawing it on walls everywhere.

Dictators tend to make it easy for you to caricature them. Hitler had his toothbrush moustache and greasy sweep of hair; Stalin was a living contradiction, presenting himself

"Europe is Getting Hot! We've Got to Move to the Western Hemisphere…" by Arthur Szyk (1944): Like a gang of hoodlums eager to make their getaway, the top Nazis [clockwise: Hitler, Goebbels, Goering and Himmler] plan escape to South America in the wake of Stalingrad and all their other setbacks. They're taking fellow fascist Franco with them, possibly because he knows the language. There's an open bag on the floor marked "Monkey Business for South America" and a plan to bring their propaganda war to the USA, but the truth is, they're finished!

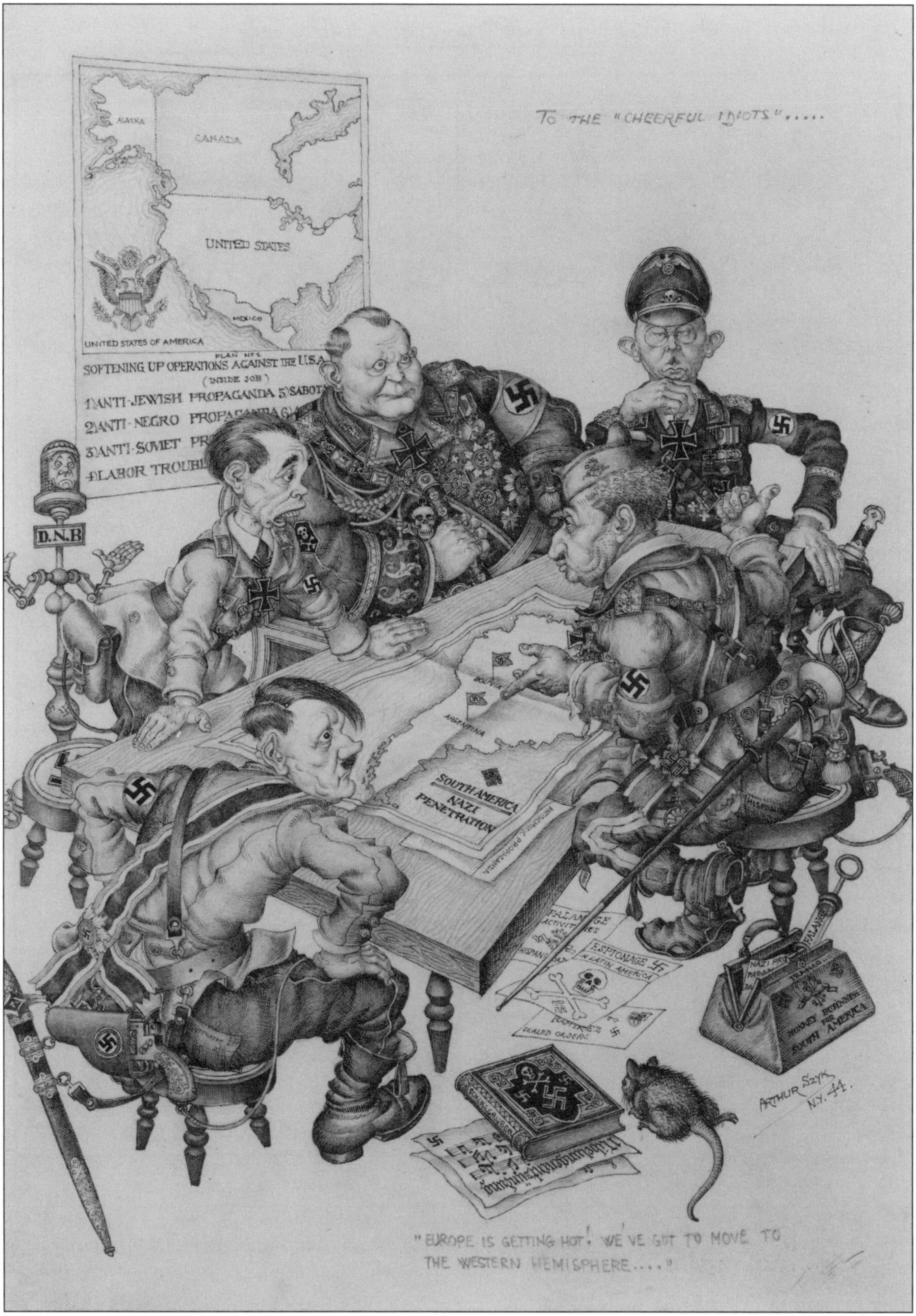
TO THE "CHEERFUL IDIOTS".....
ALASKA
CANADA
UNITED STATES
MEXICO
UNITED STATES OF AMERICA
SOFTENING UP OPERATIONS AGAINST THE U.S.A
(INSIDE JOB)
1)ANTI-JEWISH PROPAGANDA 5)SABOTA
2)ANTI-NEGRO PROPAGANDA
3)ANTI-SOVIET PRO
4)LABOR TROUBL
D.N.B
ARGENTINA
SOUTH AMERICA
NAZI
PENETRATION
ESPIONAGE
IN LATIN AMERICA
SEALED ORDERS
MONEY BUSINESS
SOUTH AMERICA
ARTHUR SZYK
N.Y. 44.
"EUROPE IS GETTING HOT! WE'VE GOT TO MOVE TO
THE WESTERN HEMISPHERE...."

Reproduced with the cooperation of The Arthur Szyk Society, Burlingame, CA

"Life in the Day of a Dictator" by Herb Block (c.1938): Block was an early campaigner against Europe's dictators in the 1930s and, through his cartoons, sought to persuade US public opinion against an isolationist stance as the threat of the dictators built up across the Atlantic. Block won the Pulitzer Prize three times and shared a fourth.

as "Uncle Joe" while radiating a force field of evil and cunning; Mussolini swaggered and strutted around.

The more they promoted themselves, the more dictators challenged cartoonists to take them down a peg or two.

So who was the most evil dictator? A good way of passing the time on a rainy Sunday is to invent your own soccer XI of tyrants. In my team, Hitler plays on the right wing, with Stalin on the left. Big, beefy Mussolini makes the ideal shot-stopping goalkeeper, with Vlad

"The Incompetent Carried by the Underlings" by Robert Osborn (1973): A malicious figurehead of power is borne aloft by the armed masses and heads for an unknown destination in this darkly brilliant drawing. Robert Osborn was working as a tutor in Austria when he witnessed a Hitler rally in 1938: "I was sickened and convinced that before us was a demon."

"Der Deutsche Michel" by Johann Richard Seel (1842): In his nightcap, Michel is an easy-going simpleton, the everyman representative of the German states. While he sleeps, he is robbed by the British Bulldog, bled dry by the Austrian diplomat Prince Metternich, lulled by a Cossack whispering sweet nothings in his ear and reduced to silence by the Pope. At the same time, France is taking the shirt off his back. To cut a long story short, the Great Powers are doing everything possible to keep him drowsy. The caricaturist is trying to warn Germans of the dangers surrounding them in pre-revolutionary Europe (prior to the 1848 revolutions)… and to wake up and defend themselves.

"I Think That Gives Me the Casting Vote" by Michael ffolkes (1963): ffolkes (real name Brian Davis) was a flamboyant figure around London, smoking "torpedo-sized cigars," drinking huge amounts of champagne and driving a large Bentley – dictator-type behavior when you come to think about it. He said his work was influenced by "classic film situations."

the Impaler a shoo-in at right-back and Franco on the left. Father-and-son combo Kim Jong Il and Kim Jong Un would be my top choice at centre-back. Ahead of them in midfield are Pol Pot, Saddam Hussein and Colonel Gaddafi, with Chairman Mao up front to head them in. Can you beat that line-up?

In compiling this book, we had to limit the selection, and if we've left out any old favorites, we apologize. There are so many, we couldn't fit them all in. Instead, we've gone with the work of some of the greatest cartoonists ever to dip their pens in acid.

Laughter confuses dictators, and knocks them off their stride. When dictators laugh, it's visibly cold and heartless, as you can see from old newsreels of Hitler, Mao or Stalin. But the laughs here come from seeing through the bluster of history's most bullying personalities and relishing their demise.

Sadly, despite cartoonists' best efforts, dictators don't appear to be going away any time soon. In fact, there seem to be as many as ever. When North Korea's "Dear Leader" Kim Jong Il died, I drew a cartoon saying,

"I think that gives me the casting vote."

"Before… and After" by Griffin (1986): Ronald Reagan promoted the image of being a strongman standing up to the world's dictators and terrorists, but this was tarnished when a Congressional Committee investigating the Arms to Iran Scandal discovered that profits from the arms sales were being siphoned off to the Contra rebels in Nicaragua.

BEFORE..

THE CAT THAT TRIED TO LOOK AT A DICTATOR.

.. AND AFTER

"The Cat That Tried to Look at a Dictator" by George Morrow (1936): Famously a cat can look at a king, but back in 1936 when dictators were at the height of their power in Europe a cat had better watch out where its gaze fell. This cartoon is a gauge of the mood of the time, and a summary of how thin-skinned and quick to anger the decade's tyrants were with their brainwashed populations eager to fall in behind them.

"Kim Jong Il… Kim Jong Dead." I thought that was all he deserved. This is the joy of skewering dictators. You don't need to show them any pity, because they never show pity themselves.

I was once beaten up by a gang of skinheads. Later on I turned my anger into a series of cartoons about skinheads. *Private Eye* magazine liked them and asked me to do a strip and call it *Yobs*. They said they would give it a short run to see how it went. It lasted 30 years—that's 30 years of sweet revenge.

This book is a pictorial history of the fightback cartoonists have led against the tyrants of history on behalf of ordinary men and women everywhere. These are drawings against all bullies who seek to destroy our lives and our dreams.

Tony Husband

THE HAGUE PEACE CONGRESS — A LAUGH FROM THE GALLERY.

"The Hague Peace Congress—a Laugh from the Gallery" by C. Hassman (1907): The shades of history's greatest despots, invaders and conquerors (including Oliver Cromwell, Ramses, William I, Hannibal, Attila the Hun, Saladin, Alexander the Great, Julius Caesar, and Napoleon) watch the peace congress from the gallery with great amusement. Perhaps they knew what was coming in 1914.

Chapter 1

TYRANTS
from Long Ago

Do tyrants pay much attention to cartoons? Napoleon claimed that the drawings of James Gillray did more than all the armies of Europe to bring him down. King Louis-Philippe of France jailed cartoonist Honoré Daumier, claiming "a caricature amounts to an act of violence." Corrupt New York politico William "Boss" Tweed perhaps put it best when he complained about cartoonist Thomas Nast: "I don't give a straw for your newspaper articles; my constituents don't know how to read, but they can't help seeing them damned pictures." Public ridicule is what dictators fear most, and what cartoonists do best. Editorial cartoons provide a necessary antidote to all the abuses heaped upon us by the powerful.

C · GALIGVLA · CÆS · AVG · IIII · RO · IMP·

Ant.temp.figurais 1196

It's said that Emperor Caligula slept with his three sisters, squandered huge amounts of money on luxury, opened a brothel in his own palace, and declared himself to be a living god. He also had plans to make his horse, Incitatus, a Consul. His motto was "Let them hate me, as long as they fear me." Aged 28, he was murdered by the Praetorian Guard in AD41, four years after coming to power. He had hardly got going really…

NERO · CLAVD · VI · CÆS · AVG · RO · IMP.

Nero reigned from AD54 to 68 and began with the best of intentions. But power quickly went to his head. He executed rivals, murdered his mother, and kicked his second wife to death. But did he "fiddle while Rome burned?" It seems he tried to save his capital, but blamed early Christians for starting the fire, probably because they were an easy target. In AD68 he committed suicide after being declared an enemy of the Roman Empire.

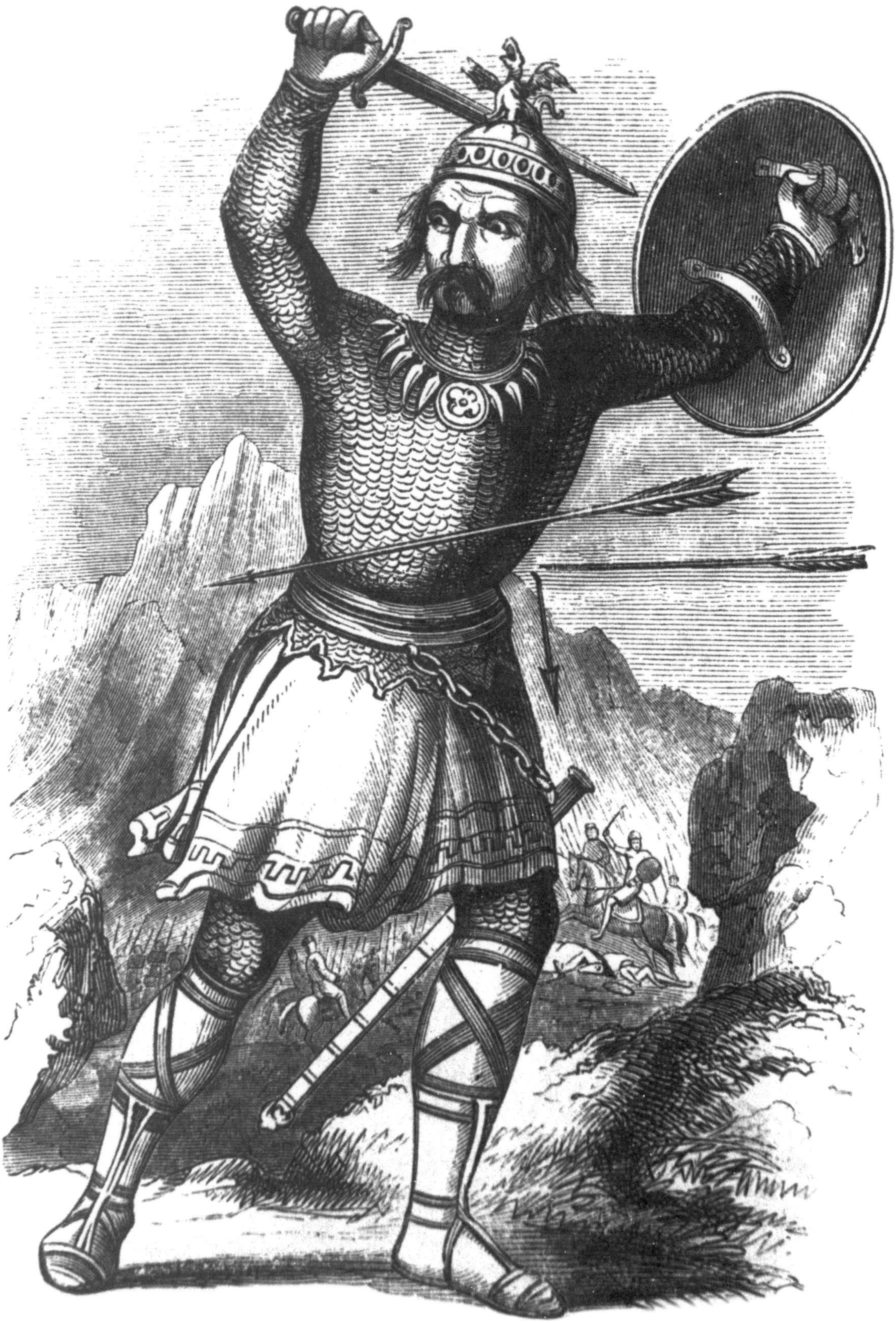

Renowned for his sadism, Tamerlane, or Timur, began life as a sheep rustler, but moved on to lead a huge horseback army into Persia, Mesopotamia, Russia, India, and Turkey, and in the direction of China. His cruelties were legion: he buried thousands of people alive or cemented them into walls; he cut prisoners in two at the waist; tens of thousands of innocents were beheaded because he liked building towers with their skulls. By the time he was done, he ruled an empire that stretched from Damascus to Delhi. Finally he fell ill at the head of a 200,000-strong army in 1405. They all prayed for him, but he could not be saved.

Opposite: Temujin was born in 1162, and by 1206 he ruled all Mongolia. That's when he acquired the name Genghis Khan, king of kings, and he went on to found the Mongol Empire, the biggest empire of all time. Khan and his armies wiped out 11 per cent of the world's population at the time—40 million people— and he was notorious for his cruelty. Genghis's empire eventually covered 12 million square miles, the size of Africa, meaning he conquered more than twice as much land as anyone else in history.

Vlad the Impaler, or Vlad Dracul, was the Voivode of Wallachia (now in Romania) and the model for Bram Stoker's Dracula. Vlad was an equal-opportunities torturer: his victims included men and women, young and old, from every religion and social class. In his domain, all crimes were punishable by impalement. Backed by the popes in Rome as "defender of the Christian faith" in eastern Europe, he murdered over 200,000 people before he was executed by the Turks in 1467.

The first Prince of Moscow to be made Czar of Russia, Ivan the Terrible, lost it when his first wife died. He started executing people willy-nilly in hideous ways, including burning at the stake, impaling, and boiling in oil. He murdered two wives as well as his eldest son. One story sums him up. In 1554, he ordered the building of St. Basil's Cathedral in Moscow and had the architect blinded so he could never create anything as beautiful again.

ABOVE: "The Pope Suppressed by Henry VIII" (1534): Henry VIII wanted a divorce from Catherine of Aragon, but Pope Clement VII was unwilling to grant it. So Henry made himself "Supreme Head in Earth of the Church of England," which cleared the way to bring in Anne Boleyn. In this picture, Henry sits on a throne using the Pope as a footstool, while the Catholic clergy quiver at the front.

LEFT: "Idol-Worship or The Way to Preferment" (1740): anonymous satire on Britain's first prime minister Robert Walpole, with his bottom exposed for an ambitious young man to kiss. A cynic might say nothing much has changed since then for those who are ambitious.

"Bombardment of all the Thrones of Europe and the Eradication of Tyrants for the Happiness of the Universe" (1792): All-singing, all-dancing cartoon from the time of the French Revolution, with members of the French National Assembly exposing their bottoms and raining freedom down upon the rulers of Europe. It's all good clean fun.

ABOVE: "The Genius of France Extirpating Despotism, Tyranny and Oppression from the Face of the Earth" by Isaac Cruikshank (1792): The French Revolution viewed from England, with Liberty holding a cat-o'-nine-tails as Louis XVI is trampled underfoot and the world's rulers attempt to flee. This was a warning to the upper classes.

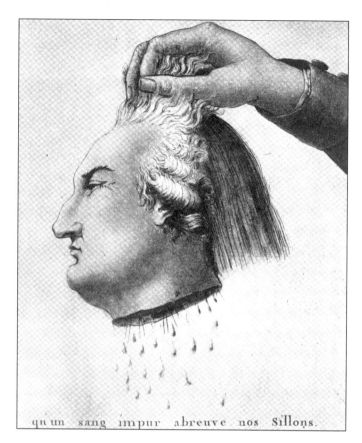

quum sang impur abreuve nos Sillons.

"Matters for Reflection for Crowned Jugglers" (1793): Beneath the severed head of Louis XVI is a line from the *Marseillaise*—"May an impure blood water our furrows." The execution didn't go smoothly. The heavy blade of the guillotine went "horribly" through the back of the king's head and jaw rather than neck. His body, "clothed in a white vest and grey silk breeches with matching stockings," was taken to the old Church of the Madeleine in Paris, vespers were said, and it was thrown on to a bed of quicklime, then covered with earth. His head had been placed at his feet.

MENE MENE, TEKEL, UPHARSIN

The Hand-Writing upon the Wall.

"My little friend Grildrig, you have made a most admirable "panegyric upon Yourself and Country, but from what I can "gather from your own relation & the answers I have with "much pains wringed & extorted from you, I cannot but con-"-clude you to be, one of the most pernicious, little-odious-"-reptiles, that nature ever suffer'd to crawl upon the surface of the Earth."

The KING of BROBDINGNAG, and GULLIVER.

Vide Swift's Gulliver: Voyage to Brobdingnag

OPPOSITE: "The Hand-Writing upon the Wall" by James Gillray (1803): Napoleon looks on in dismay as he sees the words that spell doom in the Book of Daniel appear in the sky. In this reconstruction of Belshazzar's Feast, obese Josephine, and allied French stereotypes tuck greedily into dishes marked Roast Beef of Old England, Bank of England and Tower of London, an allusion to Napoleon's intended invasion of England.

ABOVE: "The King of Brobdingnag, and Gulliver" by James Gillray (1803): Nodding to *Gulliver's Travels*, Gillray has George III in military uniform hold a tiny Napoleon in the palm of his hand and inspect him with an eye-glass. Napoleon seems to have been around 5ft 6in (1.68m), average back then, but the myth is he was tiny, giving rise to the idea of a Napoleon complex. That's the power of propaganda.

"We're in deep trouble now - he's begun to have doubts about whether or not he actually is Napoleon."

A modern take on
Napoleon from
Ray Lowry (1988),
who was a regular
contributor to
Punch, *Private Eye*
and *New Musical
Express*.

(Le Cardinal Fesch.)

La Consultation.

ABOVE: "*La Consultation*" by François Séraphin (1815): The crown is slipping off his head and Napoleon appears to be on his way out as "Le Cardinal Fesch," his favorite diplomat, takes his pulse. "Dear Cousin, how do you find my state?" "Sire, it cannot endure; your Majesty has a very bad constitution."

OPPOSITE: "Charon's Boat—or—the Ghosts of "All the Talents" Taking Their Last Voyage,—from the Pope's Gallery at Rome" by James Gillray (1807): A mad group of naked Whig politicians sets out across the River Styx in a leaky boat called the *Broad-Bottom Packet*. On the far shore, where the flames of Hell lick high, can be seen dictators Oliver Cromwell and a headless Robespierre. They're both waving their welcome.

OPPOSITE: "The Grand Coronation Procession of Napoleon I, Decr. 2d. 1804" by James Gillray (1805): The glory of the occasion is undermined by Gillray's details, such as Josephine's vast girth, a maid of honour with a black eye, and the Devil hiding behind the mask of a child next to the Pope.

Gillray fec. CHARON'S-BOAT

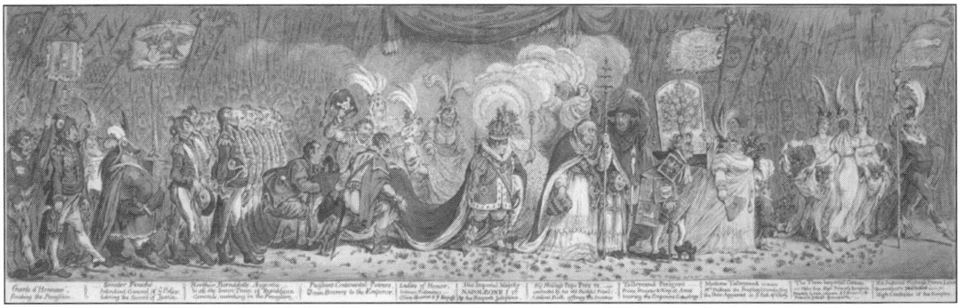

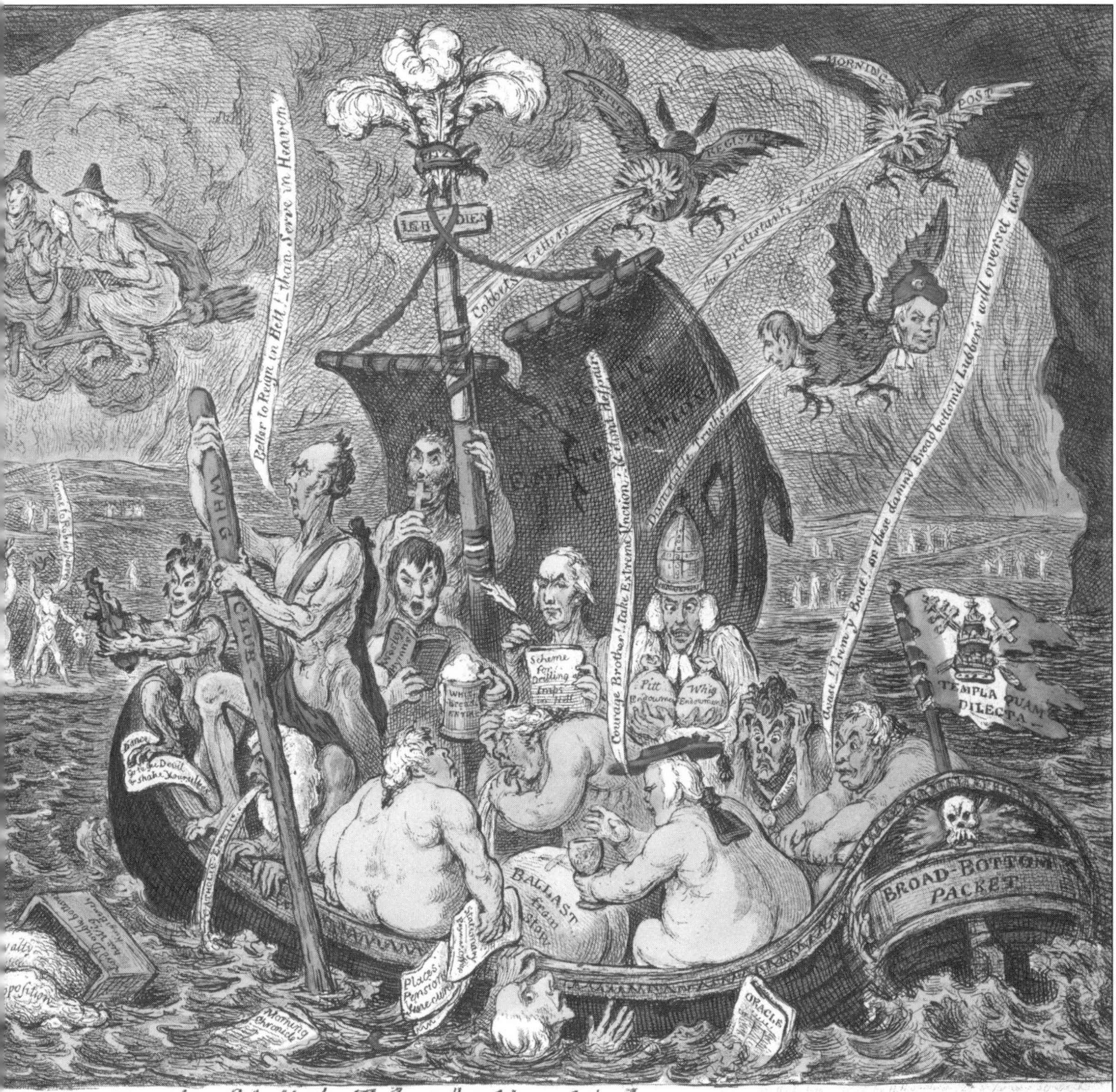

Better to Reign in Hell, than Serve in Heaven
WHIG
CLUB
Scheme for Drilling of Imps
Pitt Endowment
Whig Endowment
Courage Brother! take Extreme Unction; & dont despair
Avast! Trim y' Boat! or these damn'd Broad bottom'd Lubbers will overset us all
TEMPLA QUAM DILECTA
BROAD-BOTTOM PACKET
BALLAST from Stow
Places Pensions
ORACLE
Morning Chronicle
MORNING POST
REGISTER
Cobbett's Letters
r – the Ghosts of "all the Talents" taking their last voyage. – from the Pope's Gallery at Rome.

le Peuple Sous l'ancien Regime

"*Le Peuple Sous l'ancien Regime*" (1815): Louis XVI, a bishop, and a member of the aristocracy ride on the back of a man, who represents the people: he's blindfolded, in chains, and crawling on his hands and knees. This is intended to show how it was before the French Revolution. The bishop holds a piece of paper labeled "Inquisition," while Louis XVI whips the poor man on in the name of the Lord.

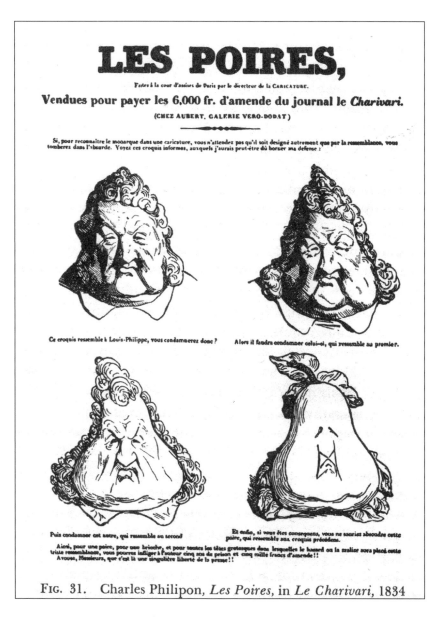

FIG. 31. Charles Philipon, *Les Poires,* in *Le Charivari,* 1834

"King Louis-Philippe Transformed into a Pear" by Honoré Daumier (1831): Daumier brilliantly re-drew Charles Philipon's original pen and blister-ink sketches of the French monarch to pay off fines which Philipon, editor of *La Caricature* magazine, had incurred in his fight for freedom of the press. Philipon was prosecuted 16 times between 1831 and 1832, spending time in prison. Pears became the symbol of the regime. Pear-shaped graffiti began to appear all over the Latin Quarter in Paris and spread out across the country. Soon the French found it impossible to think of their king without also thinking of a pear.

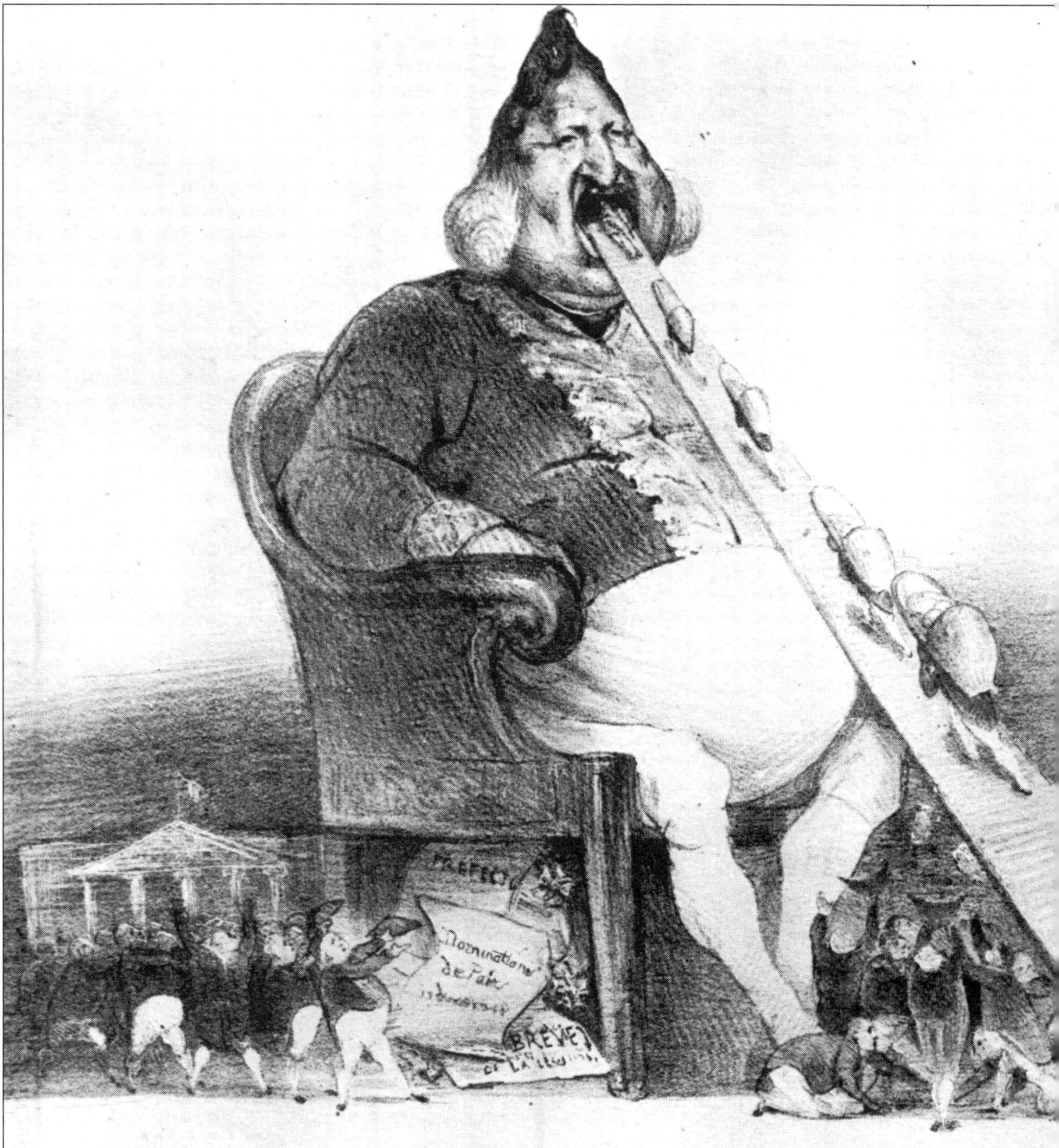
BREVET
h. Daumier

"Gargantua" by Honoré Daumier (1831): Daumier received a six-month prison sentence for depicting King Louis-Philippe as Gargantua, a grotesque giant from a scatalogical novel by Rabelais. Here, the king with his undeniably pear-shaped head sits on a giant commode excreting political favors, while servants ferry sacks of money up a huge plank into his mouth. This is the king consuming the taxpayers' hard-earned cash. The people live in a state of poverty so that the king can indulge himself and hand out privileges. Underneath the plank, merchants gather to catch any coins that are dropped. Louis-Philippe wasn't best pleased by this lithograph. It caused him to reimpose press censorship and send officials across France on an unsuccessful mission to destroy all copies.

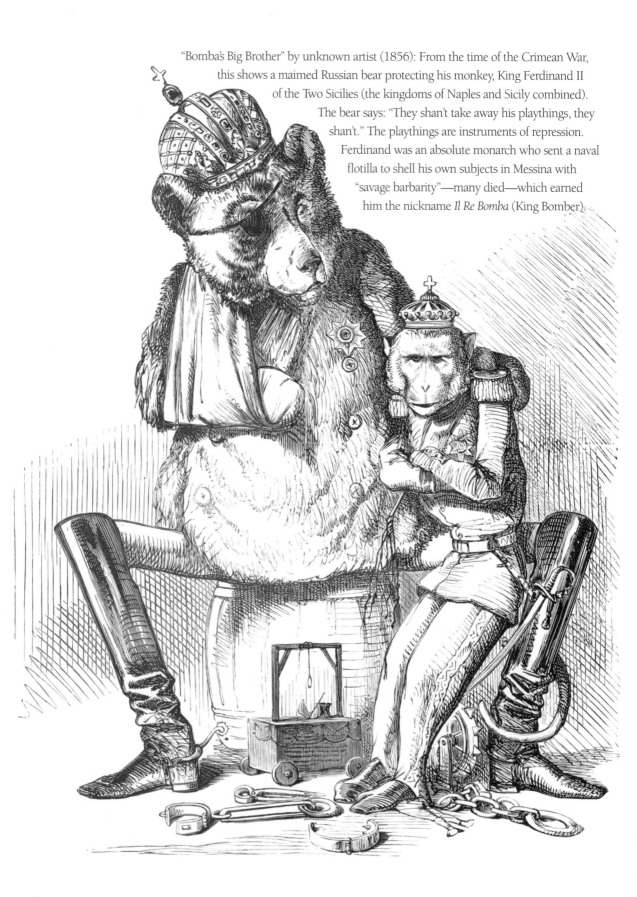

"Bomba's Big Brother" by unknown artist (1856): From the time of the Crimean War, this shows a maimed Russian bear protecting his monkey, King Ferdinand II of the Two Sicilies (the kingdoms of Naples and Sicily combined). The bear says: "They shan't take away his playthings, they shan't." The playthings are instruments of repression. Ferdinand was an absolute monarch who sent a naval flotilla to shell his own subjects in Messina with "savage barbarity"—many died—which earned him the nickname *Il Re Bomba* (King Bomber).

GEN LOPEZ THE CUBAN PATRIOT GETTING HIS CASH

LOPEZ. Well we have not Revolutionized Cuba, but then we have Got what we came for, my Comrades came for Glory, I came for Cash, I've Got the Cash, they've Got the Glory, & I suppose we're all satisfied. I'm O. P. H. for the United States again. Can't Live under a Military Despotism

"Genl. Lopez: the Cuban Patriot Getting his Cash" by John L. Magee (1850): A mocking portrait of Venezuela-born General Narciso Lopez, who led an expedition of American mercenaries to liberate Cuba from Spanish rule in 1850. After briefly occupying the town of Cardenas, they were driven out by Spanish troops. Lopez is shown fleeing Cuba with a fat bag of money.

THE GIANT AND THE DWARF.

"BRAVO, MY LITTLE FELLOW! YOU SHALL DO ALL THE FIGHTING, AND WE'LL DIVIDE THE GLORY!"

L'HOMME A LA BOULE PAR DRANER.

Tartaïfle ! je ne goutrends pas ce que j'éhrouve ! Il me sensle que je affre perdu l'équilibre, et que mon pied il affre clissé sur la poule.

En vente chez STRAUSS, 7, rue du Croissant, & chez MADRE, 20, rue du Croissant.

541 — Paris. — Imprimerie VALLÉE, 15, rue du Croissant.

"L'Homme a la Boule" by Jules Renard (Draner) (1870-1): A discomfited Otto von Bismarck, dressed as an acrobat with an Imperial Eagle on his trunks, can't understand why he's losing his balance as he attempts to roll along on the globe. The Franco-Prussian war ran from 1870 to 1871. Bismarck engineered a diplomatic crisis that lured the French into war. A coalition of German states defeated Napoleon III and captured Paris, before the nation of Germany was born out of the coalition states (as well as the warm feeling of togetherness that defeating the French had engendered).

Opposite: "The Giant and the Dwarf" by John Tenniel (1859): A louche-looking Napoleon III, Bonaparte's nephew, looks condescendingly down at little King Victor Emmanuel II of Sardinia who is urging him on to fight the Austrians. The French helped the Italians defeat the Austrians at Magenta and Solferino, but would soon choose to extricate themselves from the struggle for Italian independence. A year later, Garibaldi led his expedition into southern Italy.

"The Czar Getting Up his Little Letter of Condolence to President Garfield" by
Frederick Burr Opper (1882): Reactionary Czar Alexander III was paranoid about being
assassinated after his father was murdered in 1881, the same year that President Garfield
was shot dead by Charles J. Guiteau as he was about to board a train at the Baltimore
and Potomac Railroad Station in Washington.

OPPOSITE: "Smashed!" by Louis Dalrymple (1899): A massive
gloved fist crashes down on Emilio Aguinaldo as he rides a
rocking horse labeled "Dictatorship." Aguinaldo was the first
president of the Philippines, but his term of office came to a
sudden end when he was captured by American forces during
the Philippine–American War (1899–1901).

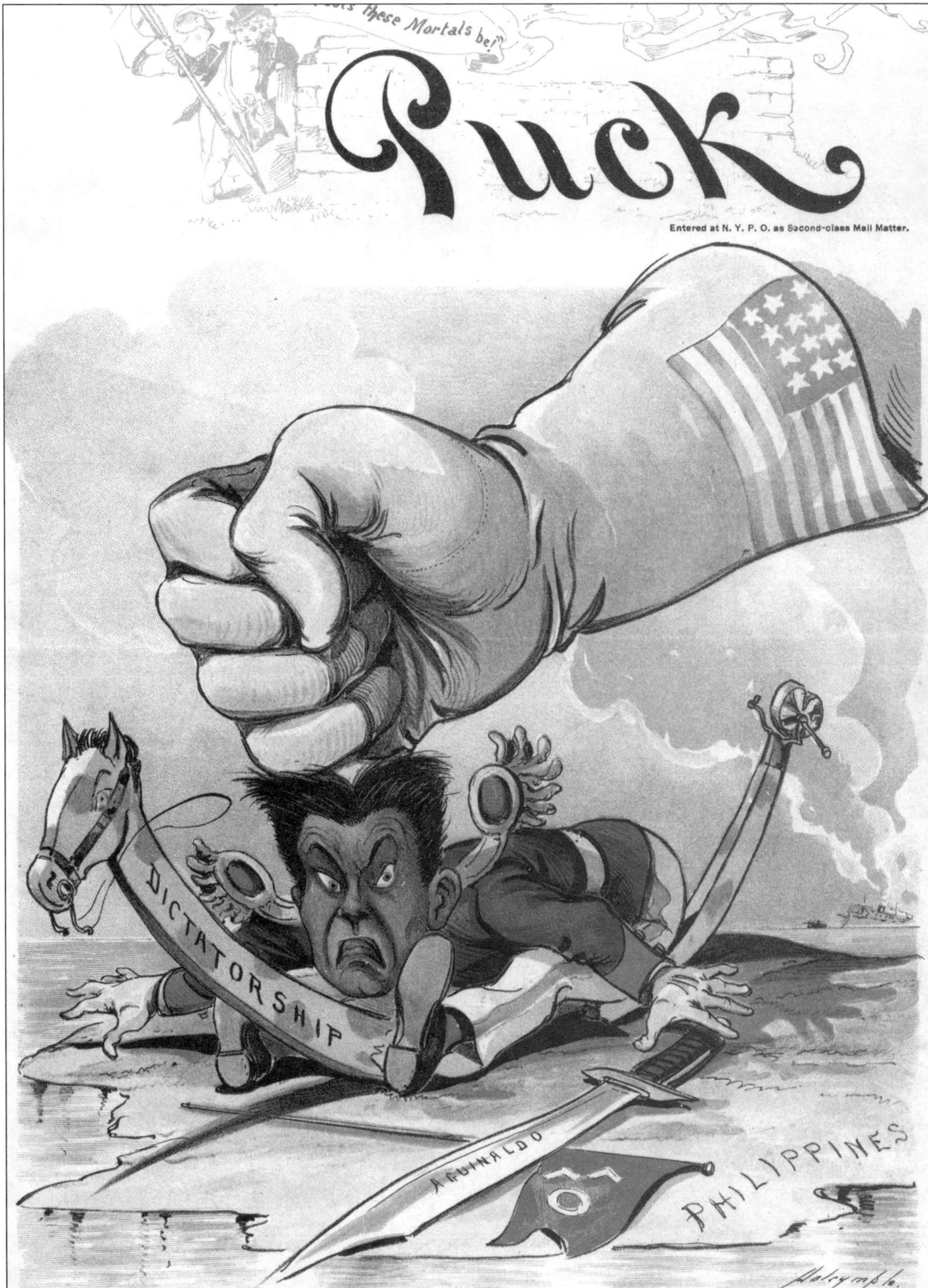
these Mortals be!
Puck
Entered at N. Y. P. O. as Second-class Mail Matter.
DICTATORSHIP
AGUINALDO
PHILIPPINES
Dalrymple.
COPYRIGHT 1899 BY KEPPLER & SCHWARZMANN.

SMASHED!

CHAINED !!

PEACE IN EUROPE IS SAFE FOR TEN YE

"Chained!" by Udo Keppler (1894): Watched by the figure of Peace reclining in a hammock, Mars the God of War is bound to rocks by the Russo-German Commercial Treaty as Russia and Germany sledge-hammer further shackles into place. It was believed the treaty would ensure peace in Europe for at least a decade, but whoever thought that had reckoned without the Greco-Turkish War of 1897 and the Macedonian Struggle (1904–8).

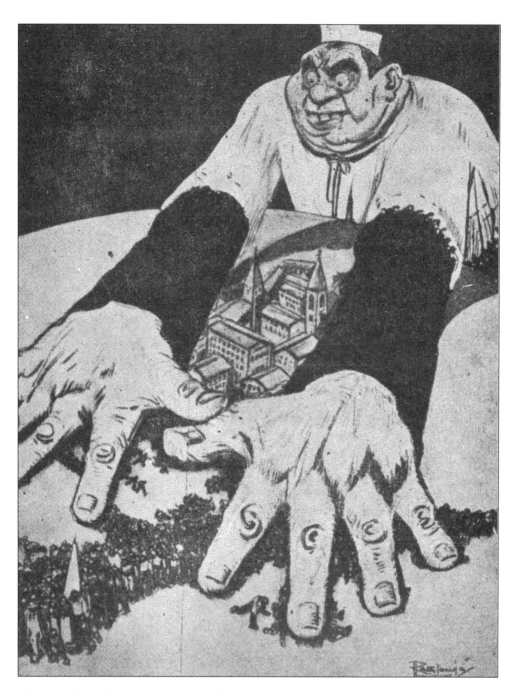

This image by Italian caricaturist Gabriele (Rata Langa) Galantara dates from around 1903 and shows the grotesque and greedy Russian giant grabbing yet more territory in a country next to Russia.

OPPOSITE: "*Un Roi Constitutionnel*" by J. J. "Coide" Tissot (1865): Slippery customer Leopold II holds on to the wealth of industrial Belgium, wary of the threat from his neighbors, represented by a jackboot for Germany and the military spats of the French. Leopold carved out his own private colony, "the Congo Free State," and turned it into a giant labor camp, making a fortune, and causing the deaths of at least 8 million innocent people.

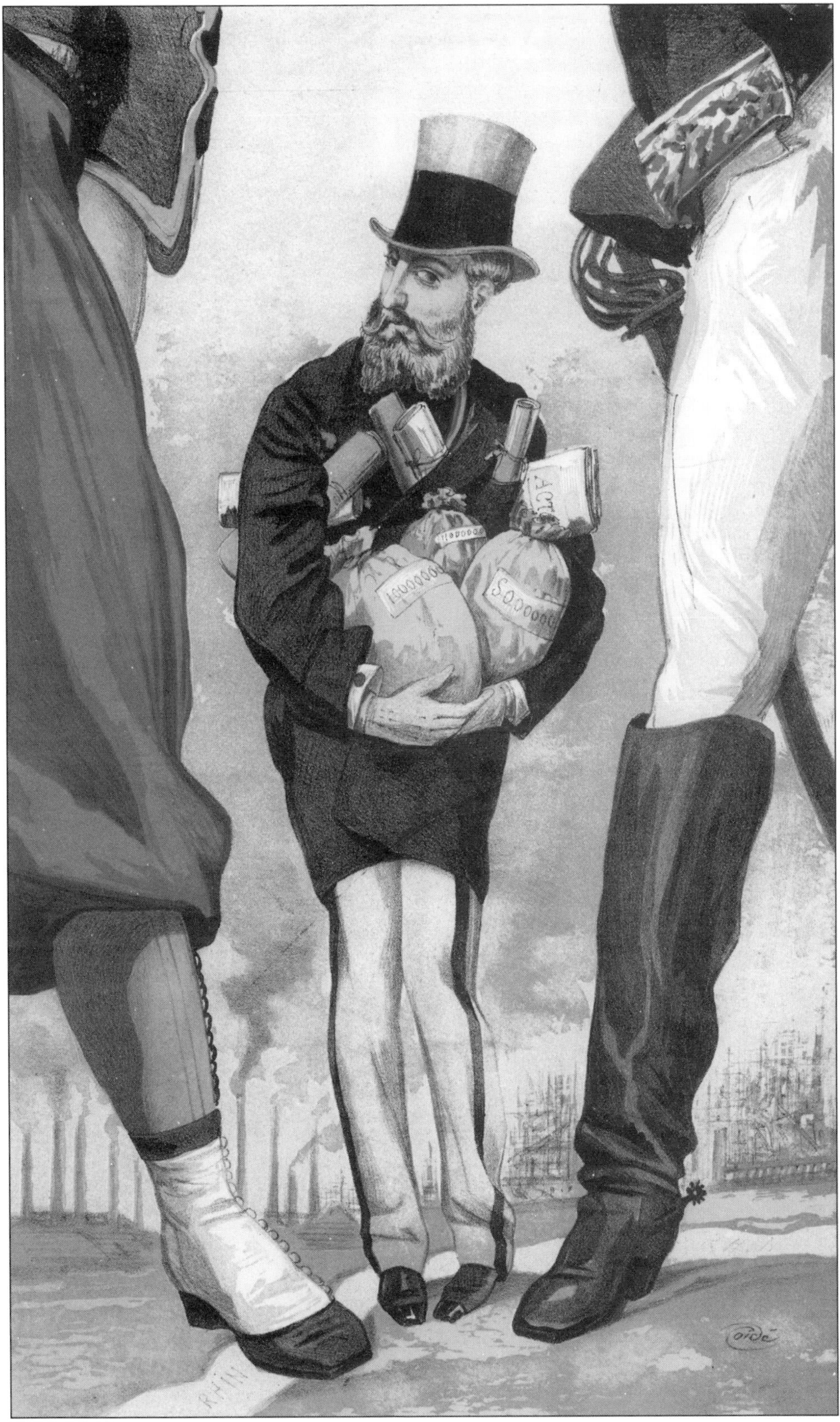
RHIN

"*Majesté… Tout est tranquille en Russe*" by Gabriele (Rata Langa) Galantara (1906): An official comes in to reassure the czar that everything is okay in the Motherland, but he seems to have walked through a hailstorm of bullets on the way. On 29 September, the Russian government ordered the maintenance of public order by "any means." This image comes from French satirical magazine *l'Assiette au Beurre*.

Louis XVI.

(Zeichnung von Wilhelm Schu[)

„Nikolaus, mach, daß du wegkommst; es ist die höchste Zeit, ich kenne den Rummel."

"Nicolas, You'd Better Get Out of Here; It's Getting Late, I recognize the signs" by Wilhelm Schulz (1906): The ghost of Louis XVI pops by to pay his respects to Czar Nicolas and to warn him about what happens to rulers who do not respect the wishes of their subjects. The grumpy-looking czar appears to be a little fazed by the lateness of the hour. This cartoon appeared in *Simplicissimus*, the German satrical magazine, which was taken over by the Nazis in the 1930s, when Schulz was re-employed as a propagandist toeing the Party line.

ÉTONNEMENT

NICOLAS. — Comme il a grandi, depuis un an !

"How He's Grown in the Last Year" by Gabriele Galantara (1906): Czar Nicholas II is astonished to find out how powerful the Russian people have become. Nicholas survived the Russian Revolution of 1905 which followed Russia's humiliating defeat in the Russo-Japanese war. But he continued to be high-handed in dealing with the problems of his native land and his family paid the ultimate price when they were executed in 1918.

OPPOSITE: "The Pan-German Moloch" by Bernard Partridge (1918): The Kaiser watches on haughtily as a diplomat called Kuehlmann is fed into the mouth of the ancient God of the Phoenicians and Canaanites. Kuehlmann made the mistake of suggesting in a speech in the Reichstag that the war could not be ended by arms alone. He was sacked by Wilhelm amid the uproar he had provoked.

THE PAN-GERMAN MOLOCH.

KAISER (*regarding the latest sacrifice*). "POOR OLD KUEHLMANN!—NEXT, PLEASE!"

"Any More Orders Today, Sire" by Will Dyson (c.1916): The figure of Kaiser Wilhelm II sits slumped before the towering winged figure of Death. The first Australian artist to visit the Front in WWI, Dyson used to preface his WWI cartoons with the following: "Mr. Dyson...responds to all the fearful pressure of this war in cartoons. He perceives a militaristic monarchy and national pride a threat to the world, to civilization, and all that he holds dear, and straightaway he sets about to slay it with his pencil… he turns his passionate gift against Berlin."

OPPOSITE: "His Spy Glass" by Sid Greene (1917): Kaiser Wilhelm peers down his telescope from a Europe in flames, hoping that the US will not join in the fight against the Fatherland. The idea was that German-American citizens were thought to be acting as successful propagandists for non-intervention. Sid Greene used to work for *The New York Evening Telegram* and *The Evening Post*; he is not to be confused with his namesake who worked for Marvel Comics.

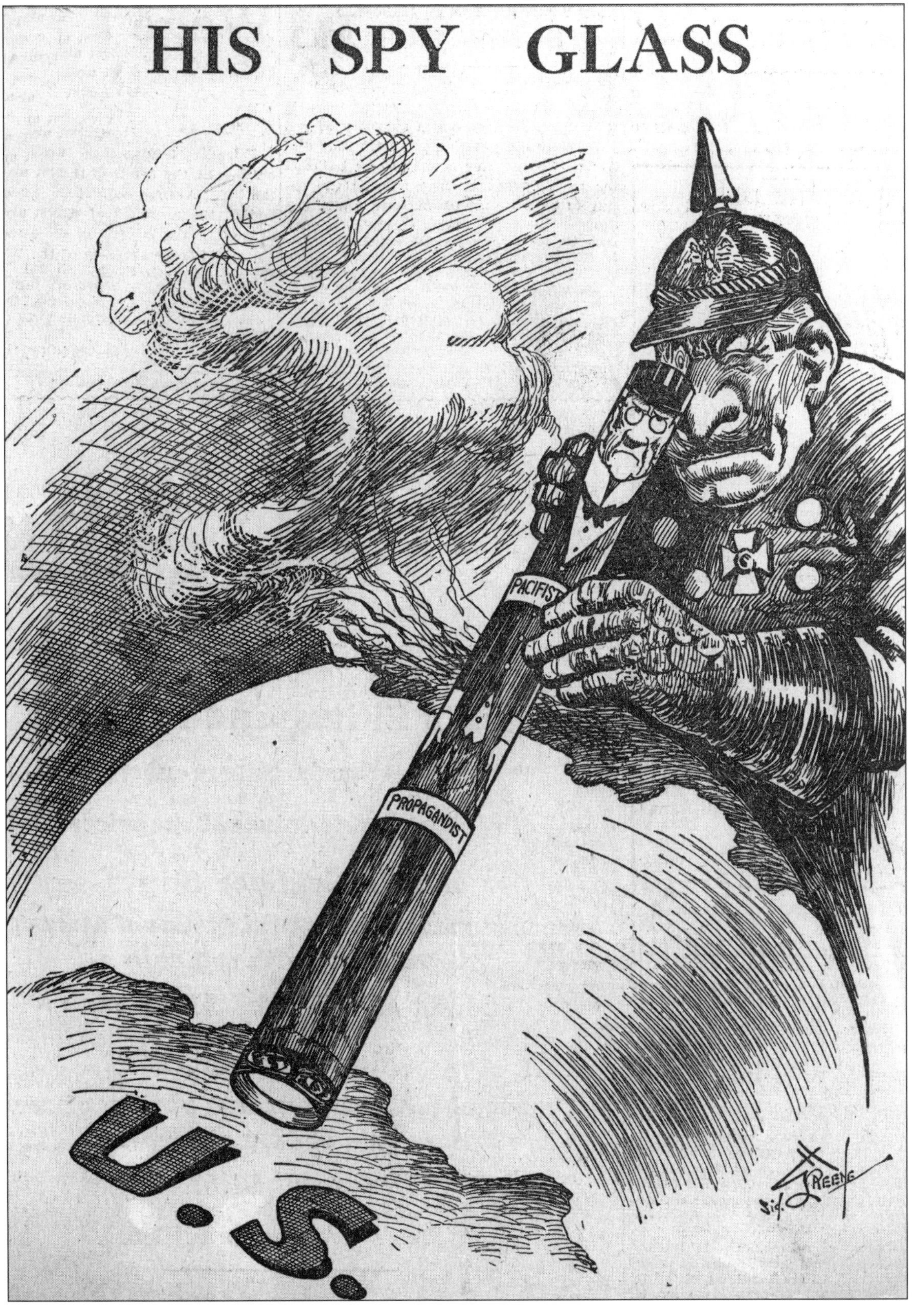
HIS SPY GLASS
PACIFIST
PROPAGANDIST
U.S.
Sid. Greene

"Trotsky and Lenin" by Erich Schilling (1921): Russia is the patient on the operating table as Trotsky and Lenin argue about the best way of curing her. Artist Erich Schilling, a regular for satirical German magazines *Kladderadatsch* and *Simplicissimus*, was critical of the Nazis until Hitler came to power. He then became a fanatical supporter, famous for his many drawings of Churchill whom he lovingly rendered as a drunk. In 1945 he committed suicide when the Third Reich came to an end.

"Enver Pasha" (1923): Enver Pasha was a member of the Triumverate Dictatorship which ran the Ottoman Empire, aka "The Three Pashas." He played a major part in the Greek genocide (1914–23) and the Armenian genocide (1915–17). Armenian recruits in the Ottoman forces were stripped of their weapons and sent into labor battalions before being executed en masse. Between 600,000 and 2.5 million died in the Armenian and Greek genocides. Throw in the 500,000 Assyrians who were also killed and the figure could be as high as 3 million. As a proportion of the population, it is thought that between half and three-quarters of the Ottoman Armenians died, which is comparable with the death rate of Jews in the Holocaust.

Imperial Caesar (by kind permission of Berlin)

This portrait of Mussolini as the propped-up bust of a Roman emperor was drawn by Philip Zec just after Italy had declared war on Britain and France in 1940. "Il Duce" thought Italy had good reason to join Germany in war: "According to the laws of Fascist morality, when one has a friend, one marches with him to the end."

Chapter 2

MUSSOLINI
Il Duce

As far as cartoonists were concerned, Mussolini was the original and the best fascist dictator. With his jutting chin, puffed-out chest and bulging eyes, they only had to exaggerate him a tiny bit in their drawings. Everything he did was larger than life. As someone said, he was "cartoon-ogenic." He was a swaggering braggart with a big mouth, who wore ostentatious uniforms with rows of medals and shiny boots that were secretly killing his feet. His life was a grand performance, but also a hollow façade. At first "Il Duce" was number one in the Dictators Top Ten—he used to look down on the others—but as his fortunes waned he seemed more and more to be the lackey of Adolf Hitler, a puppet and "Sawdust Caesar."

American Walk Over

"American Walk Over" by Leo Fontan (1933): Uncle Sam comes a cropper at the water jump in this cartoon about the fall of the dollar during the Great Depression. Watching on from Europe are John Bull, Marianne, (symbol of France), Hitler, and Mussolini. In 1933, the dollar was in crisis and the banking system in uproar. They used to say that when America sneezed, the rest of the world caught a cold: Mussolini and Hitler were waiting in the wings to dispense their patent remedy – a strong dose of fascism.

THE WAR SALAD.

MUSSOLINI. "LET ME SEE—THEY SAY 'A MISER FOR THE VINEGAR, A SPENDTHRIFT FOR THE OIL, AND A MADMAN TO STIR IT.' BUT—IS THE OIL GOING TO HOLD OUT?"

"The War Salad" by Bernard Partridge (1935): Mussolini makes his special salad out of planes and tanks and artillery at a time when the League of Nations was contemplating an oil embargo against Italy. According to an old Spanish proverb, four persons are needed to make a good salad: a spendthrift for oil, a miser for vinegar, a counselor for salt, and a madman to stir it all up…

"Little Duce ! Little Duce ! Will they love you next year as they do to-day ?"

Will Dyson, *Daily Herald*, 1936, the British Cartoon Archive, University of Kent, www.cartoons.ac.uk

"Little Duce! Little Duce! Will they love you next year as they do to-day?" by Will Dyson (1936): Propped up by the black-clad figure of War, Mussolini performs a fascist salute before adoring Italian crowds. But after Italy invaded Abyssinia (Ethiopia) in 1935, the country's relationship with the democracies was coming to a grinding halt.

RIGHT: Cartoonist KEM (Kim Evan Marengo) used to send his friends Christmas cards satirizing the international situation, and this one belonged to 1936. Based on the myth of Romulus and Remus and the founding of Rome, Mussolini suckles his own brood of fascists: Hitler, Ataturk, Metaxas, Franco, and Britain's very own Blackshirt leader, Oswald Mosley.

KEM image courtesy of Richard and Alexander Marengo

" *Little man – if you don't mind – not in my name!* "

Will Dyson, *Daily Herald*, 30.1.1936, the British Cartoon Archive, University of Kent, www.cartoons.ac.uk

LEFT: "Little man—if you don't mind —not in my name" by Will Dyson (1936): Mussolini prided himself on the idea his movement was deeply connected to classical Italian civilization. The Italians invaded Abyssinia with "tanks and flame throwers against camels and war drums." They also used poison gas and attacked Red Cross hospitals in defiance of the Geneva Convention. By May 1936 Italy had conquered Abyssinia.

THE MID-EUROPEAN TEA-PARTY.

["The March Herr and the Hatter were having tea: a Dormouse was sitting between them, and the other two were resting their elbows on it, and talking over its head."—*Alice's Adventures in Wonderland*.]

EUROPE IS ALSO PAVED WITH GOOD INTENTIONS

"Europe Is Also Paved with Good Intentions" by D. R. Fitzpatrick (1938): Fitzpatrick is commenting here on the broken promises made by Hitler and Mussolini and alluding to the road to Hell (which is also paved with good intentions). There was always a clear pecking order among the dictators of Europe. Mussolini started off as top dog in 1922, but by 1938 he was very much operating in Hitler's shadow as can be seen here. It seemed a sign of desperation when Mussolini dubbed the German-Italian alliance the "Pact of Steel", especially after it fell apart.

Opposite: "The Mid-European Tea-Party" by Bernard Partridge (1936): Adolf Hitler makes a fine March Hare from *Alice's Adventures in Wonderland* as he discusses the fate of Austria over the head of the Dormouse, representing Austria, with Mad Hatter Mussolini, who wears a natty Empire-style topper after his African adventures.

THE BORGIAS DINE TOGETHER IN ROME
"After you, my dear Alonzo!"
"No really, my dear Lucrezia, after you!"

Will Dyson, probably for the *Daily Herald*, the 1930s, the British Cartoon Archive, University of Kent, www.cartoons.ac.uk

"The Borgias Dine Together in Rome" by Will Dyson (1937): Mussolini puts in an appearance as Lucrezia Borgia, the infamous poisoner. When Goering had dinner with Mussolini at the Excelsior Hotel in Rome, he left for the station in a flowing sable coat, "something between what automobile drivers wore in 1906 and what a high-flying prostitute wears to the opera" (according to one cynical Italian observer). Goering was visibly nervous until his aides brought him a cup filled with diamonds which he played with until he calmed down. As one of his officers explained, "He had two loves—beautiful objects and making war."

"How about Hollywood Studying Mussolini?" by Herb Block (1937): In 1937 Mussolini sent his son, Vittorio, to study movie production in Hollywood, with a view to building up the motion picture industry in Italy. He stayed with producer Hal Roach. Around that time, Walt Disney invited Hitler's favorite film director, Leni Riefenstahl, to visit, and there were other right-wing propagandists who thought they could learn from the major US studios. But every time a prominent fascist arrived, the Hollywood Anti-Nazi League would be out in force protesting.

"Goering's Banquet" by Arthur Szyk (1943): The *Reichsmarschall* raises his glass to
Laval, Pétain and Darlan, members of the Vichy government, as a positively downbeat
Mussolini plays the part of waiter. Goering is shown feasting on US relief rations, while
blood drips from a list of the names of the hostages shot in France.

OPPOSITE: "The Colossus of Oaths" by Bernard Partridge (1939):
Mussolini stands in for the Greek god Helios in this image which shows
him spanning the Adriatic between Italy and Albania after Italy's invasion
of the latter. In 1942, there was a second image called "The Broken
Colossus," where he's dressed as a Roman emperor attempting to span
the straits of Gibraltar, but missing a leg after defeat in Africa.

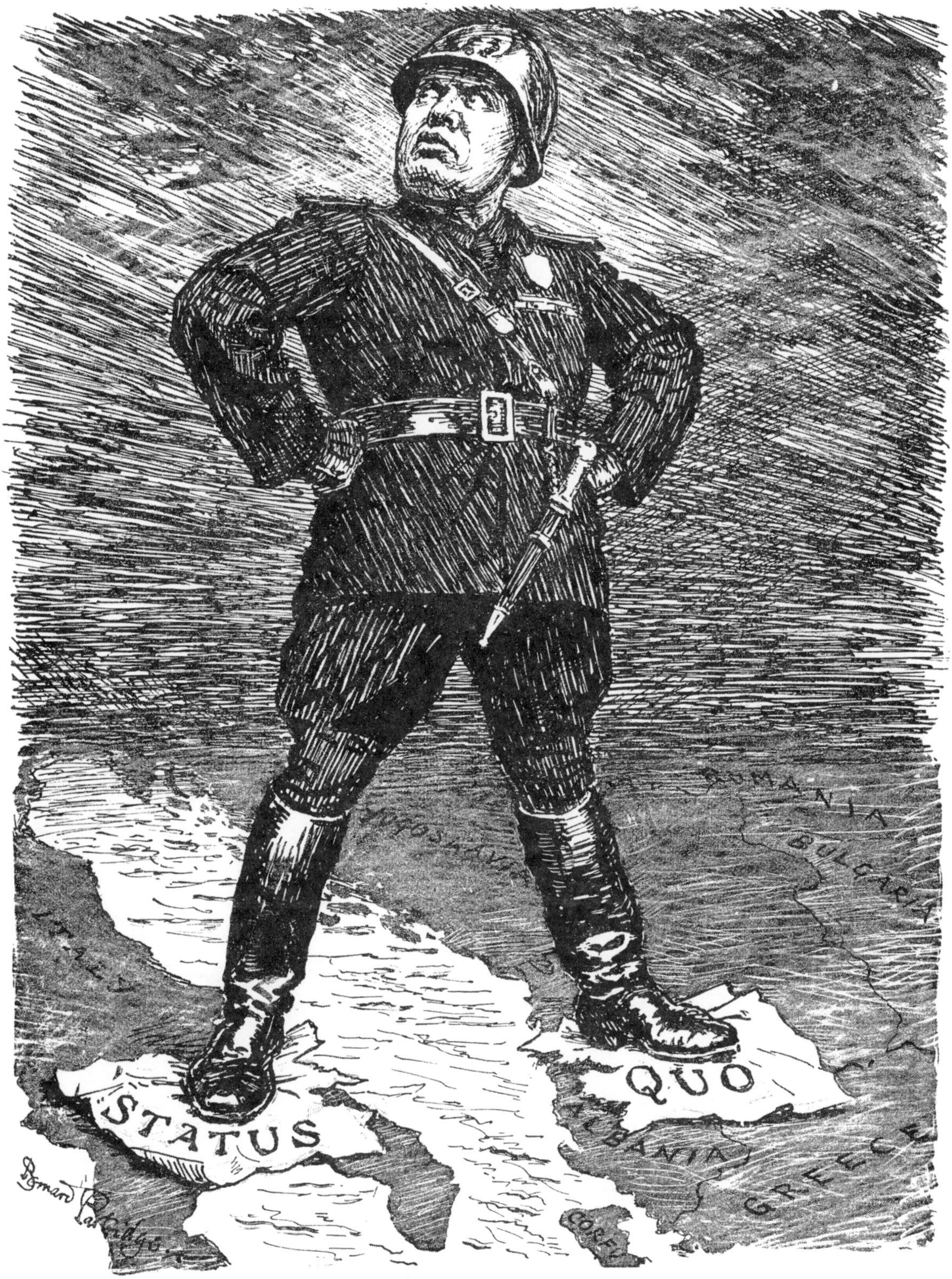
STATUS
QUO
RUMANIA
BULGARIA
ALBANIA
GREECE
CORFU

THE COLOSSUS OF OATHS

HUMPTY DUMPTY AND THE ROMAN WALL

"Humpty Dumpty and the Roman Wall" by E. H. Shepard (1940): Goebbels pulls Humpty Mussolini toward a crash landing on the German side of the wall when he might have been better off with a soft landing on Allied soil. Italy joined the war on the side of the Germans in 1940. Mussolini assumed it was only a matter of time before Britain was defeated and the Axis Powers ruled the whole of Europe. A costly mistake!

THE MAN OF STRAW

"It seems ages since I scared anybody."

"The Man of Straw" by E. H. Shepard (1941): Mussolini was always the butt of British jokes about his military prowess. When the British threatened to overrun Libya, Mussolini had to ask the Germans for help. In three months, the Italians had lost 20,000 soldiers killed or wounded and 130,000 had been taken prisoner. When Rommel arrived in North Africa, the Axis Powers had a new lease of life, managing to hold out until early in 1943.

"He Who Laughs Last, Laughs Best" by Clifford Berryman (1942): The Sphinx watches the progress of the war in North Africa, which swings backward and forward until the Axis Powers find themselves on the retreat, which is clearly to the liking of the Sphinx, which has ceased to be inscrutable.It's all a bit *Benny Hill*.

OPPOSITE: Voted out of power by his own Fascist Council, Mussolini handed his resignation in to the king. He had actually been visited by Hitler in Italy on July 18, 1943. The *Fuehrer* was trying to get "Il Duce" to buck up, but he was groggy, unshaven and overwhelmed, seemingly incapable of action. Being a dictator can be very exhausting…

Marry in haste . . . repent at leisure.

With the Allies in Sicily, and his country weary of a lost war, the Duce, for want of a better home, resigned and fled to the uneasy bosom of his Fuehrer.

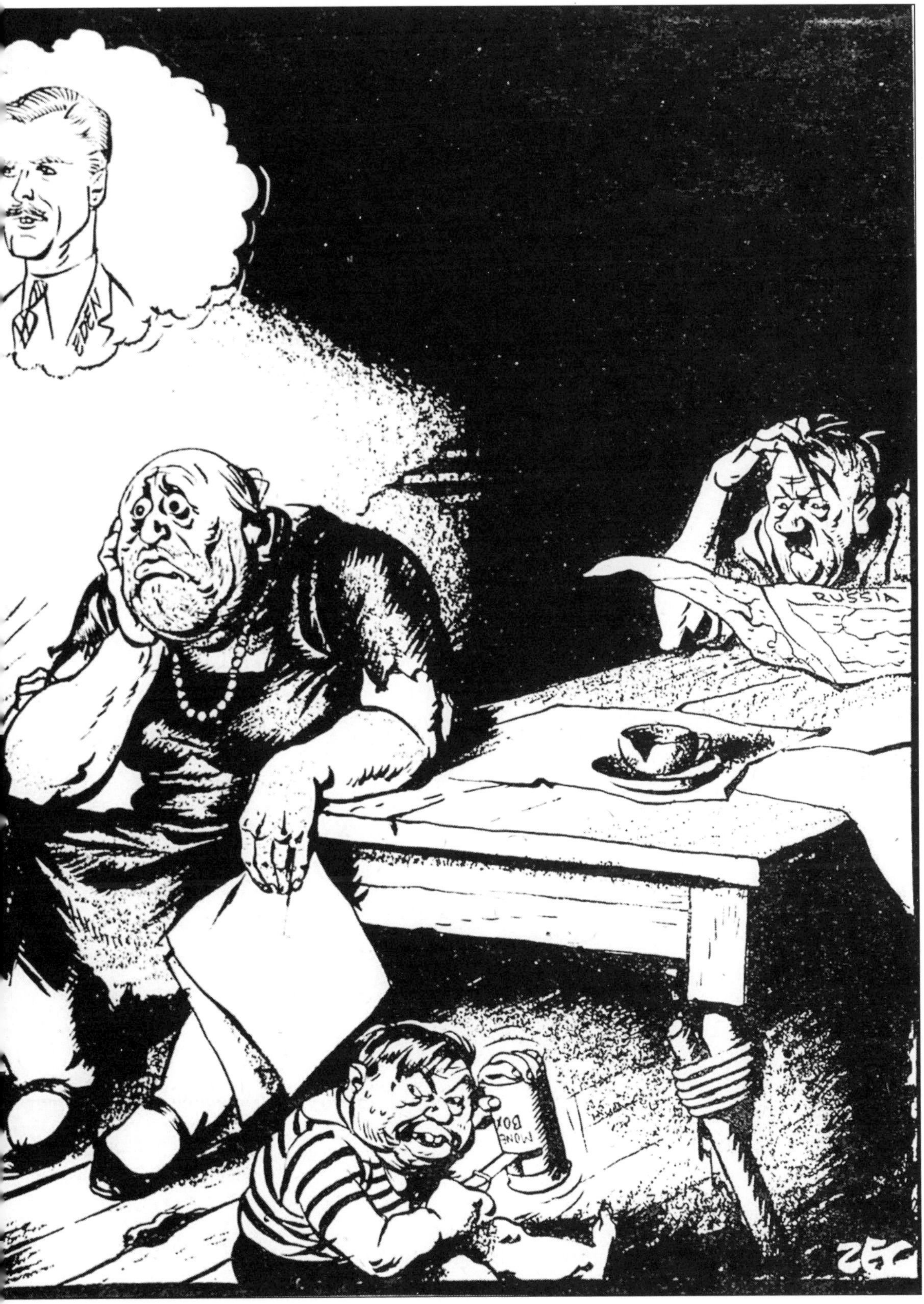
EDEN
RUSSIA
MONEY BOX
ZEC

"11 Ships Sunk off Italy" by Willard Combes (1943): A third of the Italian merchant navy was interned after Italy declared war but, by September 1942, half of the remainder had been sunk, although replacements were on their way. The normal Italian supply route to Libya went miles around the coast to avoid being caught on the open sea by British aircraft, ships and submarines based at Malta, but still the losses stacked up.

OPPOSITE: "Mussolini" by Jose Ozon (1944): This is the surrender of Mussolini as pictured by Brazilian artist Ozon in Italian futurist style. It makes a nice change to see "Il Duce" raise his arms in surrender, rather than the fascist salute. After being rescued by the Germans and taken to Bavaria, Mussolini founded the Italian Socialist Republic of Salo, a puppet dictatorship. He died with his mistress Clara Petacci on April 28 1945 in a village in northern Italy, summarily executed by partisans two days before Hitler killed himself in his bunker. Their bodies were strung from a lamp-post.

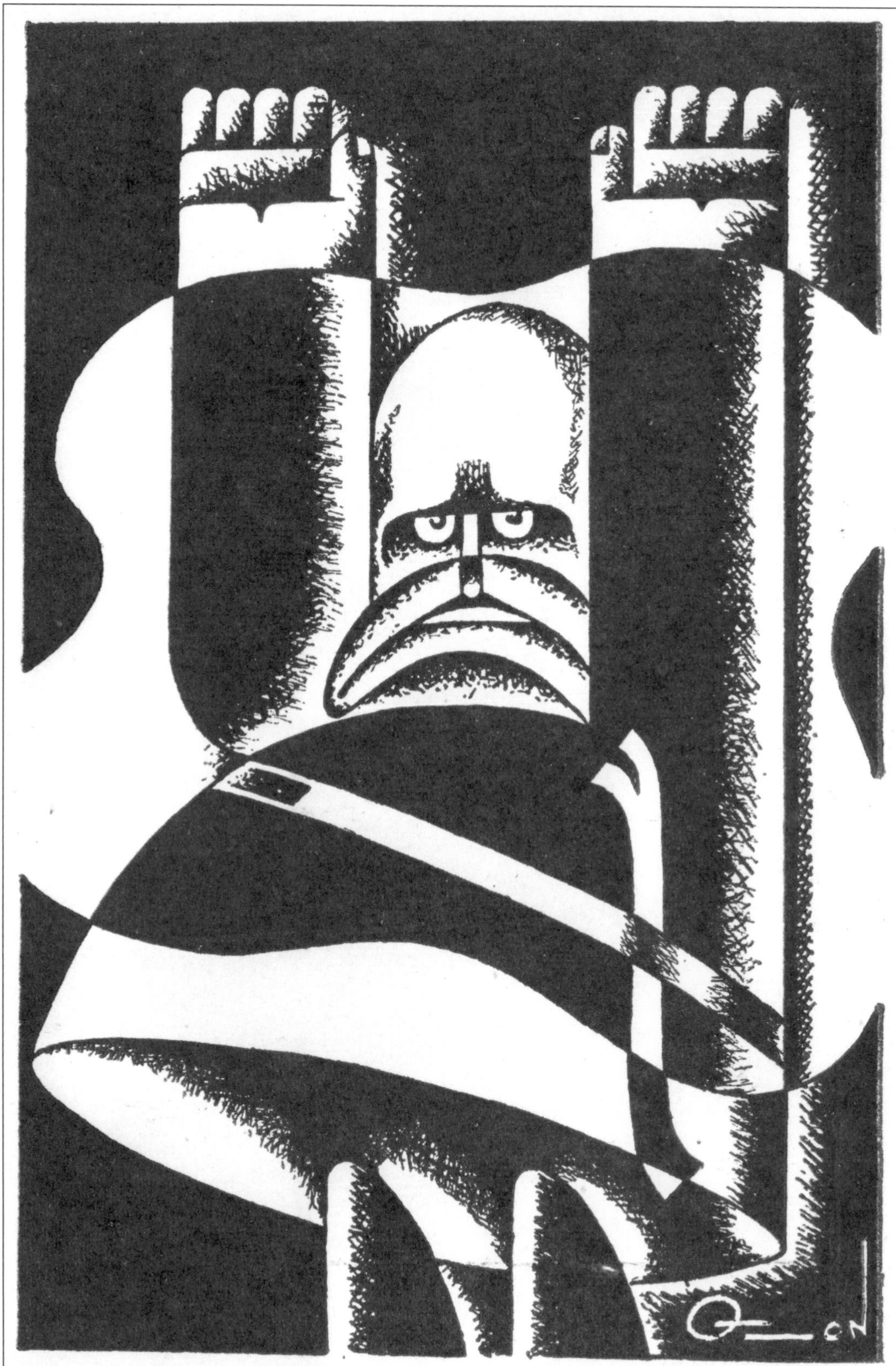

BALKAN & DISTRICT RAILWAY

THE RIVAL BUSES

LIBERTY HOTEL
COMFORTABLE ACCOMMODATION

"The Rival Buses" by E. H. Shepard (1947): In this early Cold War cartoon, Uncle Joe appears as one of those seedy greeters who directs you to "a little hotel I know, very nice place." Bulgaria and Hungary look doomed.

Chapter 3

STALIN
The Red Czar

"Regarding Stalin [I must say that] although he liked cartoons and always paid a lot of attention to them, he wouldn't allow jokes about himself... in 1925, I made a friendly drawing of him; it was returned to me with the urgent injunction: 'Not to be published.'" Thus wrote Boris Yefimov, Stalin's favorite cartoonist. Stalin was one of a tiny handful of globally recognized faces in the 1930s and 1940s. Flattering portraits of him hung everywhere in Russia and history books were rewritten to record his myths. Stalin may mean "Man of Steel," but cartoonists were obliged to draw him with feet of clay. As Yefimov said, "No matter how strong and frightening the enemy might be, when you laugh at him, the fear goes away."

THE CHEF'S PLAT DU JOUR

"The Chef's Plat du Jour" by Sidney Strube (1943): The Red Army steamrollers fleeing Germans after Stalingrad as assorted Nazis simmer on the stove. Sidney Strube grew up in a pub called the Coach and Horses on the Charing Cross Road, London. He was patriotic and wore a bowler hat. In 1934, he appeared alongside David Low and Percy Fearon as an exhibit at Madame Tussauds, which indicates the celebrity status of cartoonists back then.

"The Bolsheviks Writing a Reply to
the Englishman Curzon" (1923):
Lord Curzon is seen as a pompous
representative of the English bourgeoisie,
while of course the Bolshevik leaders
come from the "new breed of socialist
politician." Among the happy throng
are Stalin, Trotsky, Kamenev, Bukharin,
Litvinov and Zinoviev. There is no hint of
the rivalries to come.

"Mona Lisa with a Moustache" by Herb Block (1939): A portrait of the enigmatic Josef Stalin with Hitler, Mussolini and Franco as well as Chamberlain and Churchill. They're all trying to work him out. Stalin was up there with the very worst of dictators. He killed over 20 million people; at least one million were executed for political offences. He spent many evenings signing death warrants and liked to instill fear in those around him.

LEFT: "The Prussian Tribute in Moscow" (1939): Published in Warsaw's *Mucha* weekly and with a caption written in archaic, 16th-century Polish, this cartoon refers to an ancient treaty which ended war between Poland and Prussia. But now allegiance seems to be owed to Moscow, as Von Ribbentrop can be seen kissing Stalin's hand

WONDER HOW LONG THE HONEYMOON WILL LAST?

ABOVE: "Wonder How Long the Honeymoon Will Last?" by Clifford Berryman (1939): Legendary US cartoonist Clifford Berryman added his voice to the widespread mockery of the Russo-German, non-aggression pact. There were quite a few cartoons of marriage between Hitler and Stalin. Stalin always seemed to be the bride.

LES AMANT

par **Ralph**

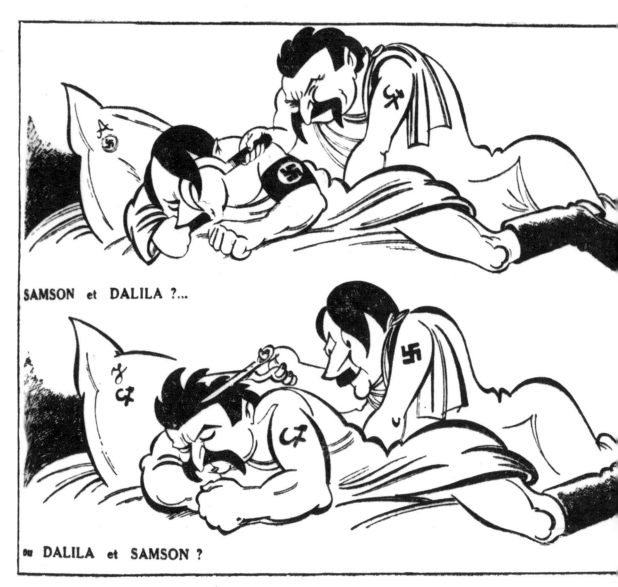

SAMSON et DALILA ?...

ou DALILA et SAMSON ?

"Les Amants Terribles" by Ralph Soupault (1936): *Les Amants Terribles* was a 1936 French film adaptation of Noel Coward's *Private Lives*. The plot revolves around a divorced couple who, while honeymooning with their new spouses, discover they're staying in adjacent rooms at the same hotel. This cartoon is a more stomach-turning affair, with classical and biblical allusions, and Stalin looking revoltingly coy as he contemplates the Reichsmarks he'll receive.

"Rendezvous" by David Low (1939): Hitler and Stalin seem to be circling each other in a gruesome *danse macabre* as a dead soldier lies stretched out between them. People were stunned at the alliance of Germany and the USSR. For sheer cynicism on both sides, it was a deal which has probably never been surpassed.

IN THE BALKAN WEB

"In the Balkan Web" by E. H. Shepard (1941): Hitler the spider has had it easy up until now preying on the little creatures like Greece, Yugoslavia, Hungary, Romania and Bulgaria. They've been easy to gobble up, but now big fat Uncle Joe is bouncing across his web toward him and it's all about to change.

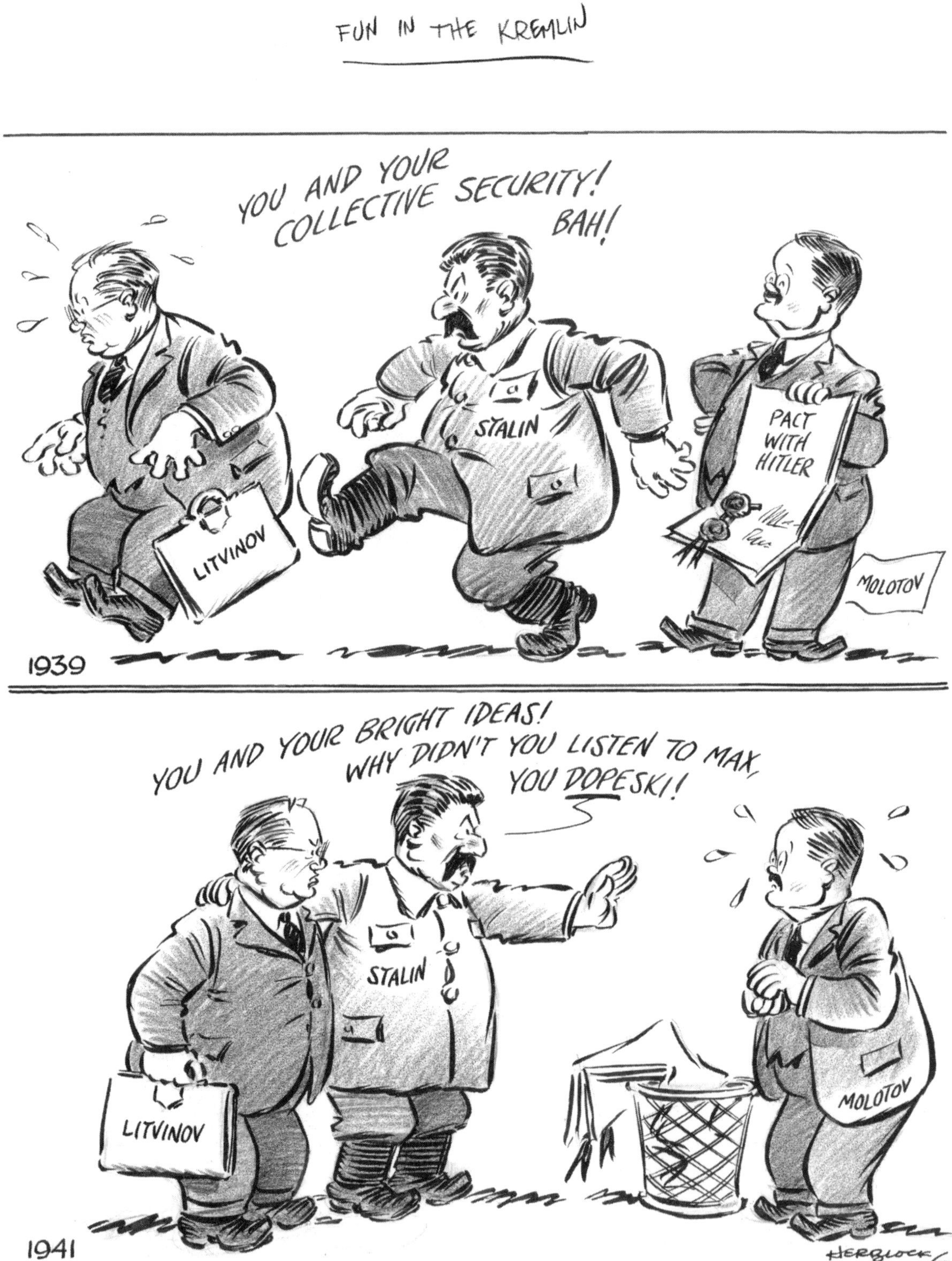
FUN IN THE KREMLIN
YOU AND YOUR COLLECTIVE SECURITY! BAH!
STALIN
PACT WITH HITLER
LITVINOV
MOLOTOV
1939
YOU AND YOUR BRIGHT IDEAS! WHY DIDN'T YOU LISTEN TO MAX, YOU DOPESKI!
STALIN
LITVINOV
MOLOTOV
1941
HERBLOCK
NEA Service, Inc.

LEFT: "*Teoria e Practica*" (undated): In this propaganda postcard from World War II, Stalin stands on a huge copy of *Das Kapital* stuffed with the bodies of victims of communism. Having performed a rapid about-face following their recent alliance with the USSR, the Germans printed this piece of black propaganda in Spanish.

RIGHT: "Dr. Sisyphus" by Bernard Partridge (1943): *Punch* cartoonist Partridge takes inspiration from the writings of Josef Goebbels: Stalin is a boulder he cannot push uphill. The Germans had failed to appreciate the unending nature of the task of taking on Russia.

OPPOSITE: "Fun in the Kremlin" by Herb Block (1941): All change at the Kremlin as Molotov is suddenly out of favor and Litvinov becomes the blue-eyed boy again now that Germany has invaded Russia.

DR. SISYPHUS

"The ascent is stony and laborious, but it must be mastered as otherwise everything has been in vain and everything is lost.—*From an article by Goebbels.*

„Ich möchte dir keine Hindernisse in den Weg legen – wir könnten uns sonst entzweien . . ."

"Border Issues" (1943/4): In this piece of German propaganda from the magazine *Kladderadatsch*, Churchill is saying to Stalin: "I wouldn't like to put any obstacles in your way—otherwise we'll never be able to get away from each other." With his round jowly face, Churchill is a difficult person to draw really well, even though he looked like nobody else. The Nazis usually liked to draw him as a portly, maudlin drunk.

In this image from 1943 by Philip Zec, a bear that looks uncannily like Stalin has a trophy of Hitler mounted on its wall. This is a mocking reassessment of the doomed position of the German Army on the Eastern Front.

"We have taken up new positions on the Eastern Wall."
Nazi Radio.

Hurled back from Stalingrad, German troops could only wait as the Red Army pre- pared for its final drive.

THE TROUBLES OF TITO

"I am the Evil Demon Russia;
I mean to holdyer and to crushyer."

"I am the Spirit of the West;
My fairy wand will make you blest."

"The Troubles of Tito" by Illingworth (1949): Stalin and the spirit of the West rival each other for President Tito's affections. Tito organized the most effective anti-Nazi resistance in Europe, but would not play ball with the USSR. Ten years after his death in 1980, Yugoslavia fell apart. Tito is said to have been responsible for the deaths of nearly 600,000 Yugoslavians, but he was viewed as "good" in the West because he opposed Russia.

OPPOSITE: "Davy Joe" by Illingworth (1949): By the late 1940s, the Soviet submarine fleet was the largest in the world, and considered a potential menace to Western shipping. "Davy Joe" is a slightly labored reference to Davy Jones' Locker.

DAVY JOE

[Alarm has been expressed in the House of Commons at the rapid increase in the Russian submarine fleet.]

"Room for Brains?" by Lute Pease (c.late-1940s): Clutching his next Five-Year-Plan, Stalin inspects the head of the Russian bear to see if he can locate grey matter. This cartoon comes from the honeymoon period after World War II when some people in the West still believed that Stalin might be interested in helping to rebuild democracy across the world. It is perhaps naive about Stalin, and certainly patronizing about the Russians.

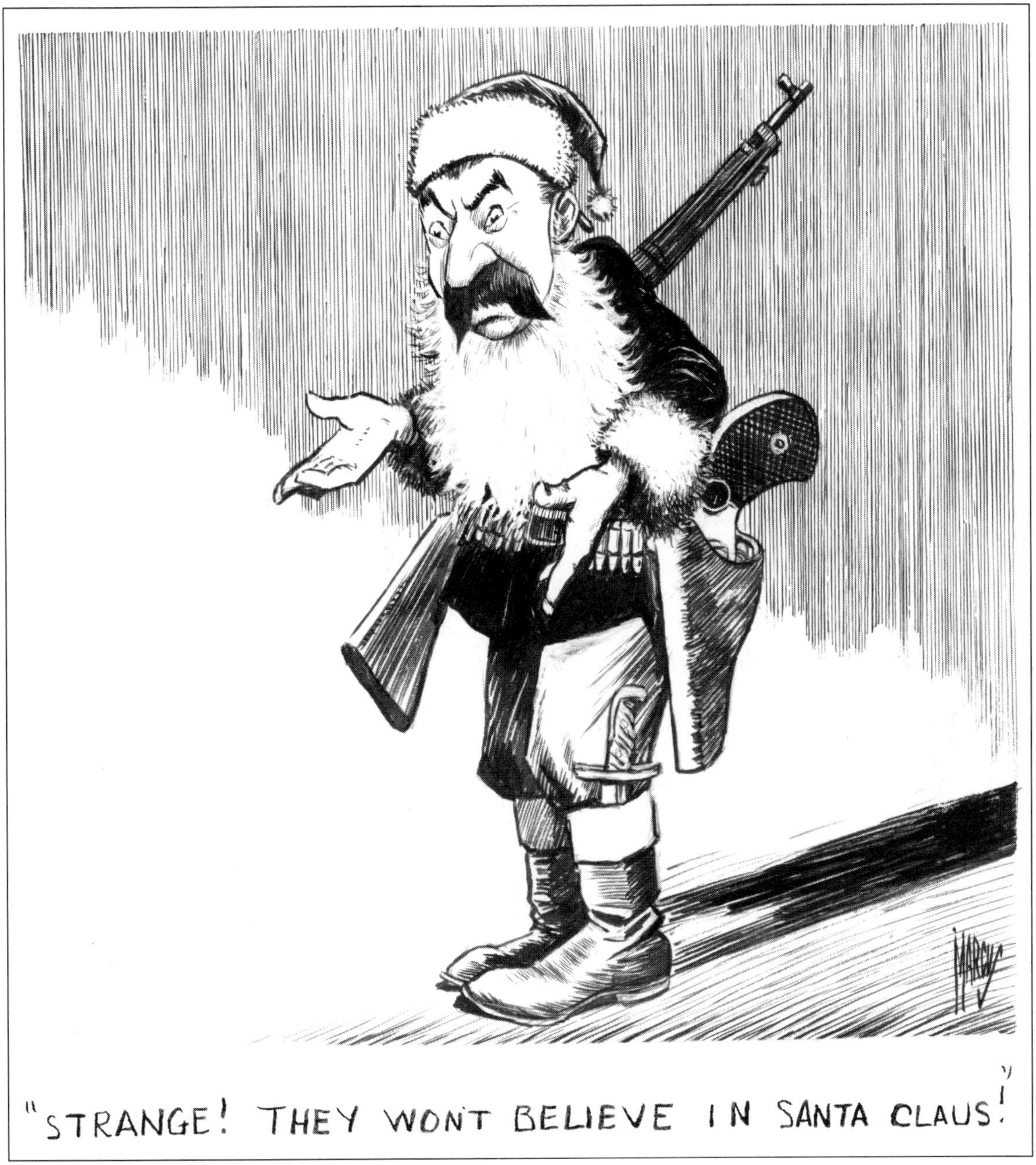
MARCUS
"STRANGE! THEY WON'T BELIEVE IN SANTA CLAUS!"

By permission of the Marcus family

"Strange! They Won't Believe in Santa Claus!" by Edwin Marcus (c.1946): Uncle Joe shouldn't have armed himself to the teeth when he came to the party dressed as Santa Claus. The West was sceptical about Russian claims to be a peaceful nation just after the war.

"Want to Come In and Be Counted, Joe?" by D. R. Fitzpatrick (1951):
Four-Power talks were held over disarmament between the United States,
Britain, France and the USSR. But the mistrust toward Stalin was intense. On
November 7, 1951, President Truman used a radio and television address to
call on the Soviet Union to agree to a new disarmament plan. In this picture
Stalin is carrying atom bombs to supplement the day-to-day weaponry.

"Welcome to Moscow!" by Jerry Costello (1952): Contrasting life
in the USSR with the USA, the Statue of Tyranny stands in place
of the Statue of Liberty in Russia's capital city. A jolly-looking
Stalin holds aloft a ball and chain in his right hand, with a fat
copy of Marx tucked under his arm. By 1952, the goodwill
engendered by victory in World War II was beginning to run out
and the Cold War was about to enter the deep freeze.

ST. LOUIS POST-DISPATCH

THE FORGOTTEN MAN

MAY. 11. 1953

"The Forgotten Man" by D. R. Fitzpatrick (1953): An empty picture frame marked "Stalin" lies discarded in a garbage can outside the Kremlin, reflecting the rapid de-Stalinization which took place after his demise in March 1953. Cartoonists never worry about shading over into *Schadenfreude*. When Stalin lay dying, his staff were too frightened to enter his room and disturb him, so medical assistance was fatally held up.

"Collapse of the Stalin Colossus" by Illingworth (1956): The statue is about to fall heavily on the people below. The collective leadership that replaced Stalin in 1953 introduced a process of de-Stalinization in the Soviet Union, dismantling the institutions that had kept him in power, such as the Gulag labor camps. Here Illingworth references the destruction of Stalin's statue in Budapest by anti-Soviet protestors during Hungary's October Revolution.

The Germany That Never Learns!

"The Germany That Never Learns!" by Philip Zec (1940): One of the best ways of putting down dictators is to suggest that they are not the intrepid leaders of men they consider themselves to be, but are merely repeating the mistakes of their foolish predecessors.

Chapter 4

HITLER
The Fuehrer

Adolf Hitler was not a particularly striking-looking individual, but he did possess a toothbrush moustache and cow's lick hair which could be used by cartoonists to "Hitlerize" almost anything, e.g. the charging horse on page 95. New Zealand-born cartoonist David Low drew Hitler for decades and chose to portray him as a harmless fool rather than as a dangerous monster. As he put it, "No dictator is inconvenienced or even displeased by cartoons showing this terrible person stalking through blood and mud. That is the kind of idea about himself that a power-seeking world-beater would want to propagate. What he does not want to get around is the idea that he is an ass, which is really damaging…"

"The Grim Reaper" by Georges, 1933: Prescient image by Georges that appeared in *The Nation*, New York on April 4, 1933, suggesting the terrible reality that lay behind Hitler's mask. Only 44 per cent of the electorate voted for the Nazis in Germany in 1933, but Hitler's forces still brutally subverted democratic procedure to seize total power. By the end of the year, trade unions had been banned, along with all other political parties.

THE GERMAN MAZEPPA.

"AWAY! AWAY! MY BREATH WAS GONE,
I SAW NOT WHERE HE HURRIED ON. . . ."

"The German Mazeppa" by E. H. Shepard (1933): By 1933, Hitler was chancellor of Germany. This cartoon is based on a poem by Byron about a Ukrainian Cossack, Ivan Mazeppa, who had an affair with a countess. Her incensed husband strapped Mazeppa naked to a wild horse and whipped the animal into a gallop so it disappeared over the horizon. The poem described the trauma of Mazeppa's journey into the unknown.

The Furtwängler Resignation

Orpheus in Germany "Legend says that once I used to subdue the savage beasts — but they went blond beasts!"

Will Dyson, *Daily Herald*, 1934, the British Cartoon Archive, University of Kent, www.cartoons.ac.uk

Doctor Mandate: "Say ninety-nine!"
(Nazis claim a full ninety-nine per cent. majority for Hitler.)

Will Dyson, probably for the *Daily Herald*, January 1935, the British Cartoon Archive, University of Kent, www.cartoons.ac.uk

"Doctor Mandate: 'Say ninety-nine!'" by Will Dyson (1935): In the run-up to the plebiscite that would return the Saar region with its coal mines into German hands from the French, the Nazis were accused of running a "reign of terror." Following a mix of "cajolery, brutal pressure, intimidation, espionage, denunciations, kidnappings and relentless surveillance," the Nazis had the result they wanted, 99 percent, or so they claimed. Dyson captures the moment as Hitler, Goebbels, and Goering help announce the result."

OPPOSITE: "The Furtwängler Resignation" by Will Dyson (1934): This cartoon shows Nazi oompah music crushing High Art as conductors race off in the background. Conductor Wilhelm Furtwängler welcomed the Nazis when they came to power because he thought it would mark a return to "German values." He saw himself as a defender of Germany's glorious musical heritage, but refused to get rid of Jewish musicians. In 1934 he was banned from conducting Hindemith's opera *Mathis der Maler*, and subsequently resigned from the *Reichsmusikkammer* and Berlin Opera. (If you can't read Dyson's handwriting, Orpheus in Germany is remarking, "Legend says that once I used to subdue the savage beasts—but they weren't blond beasts!")

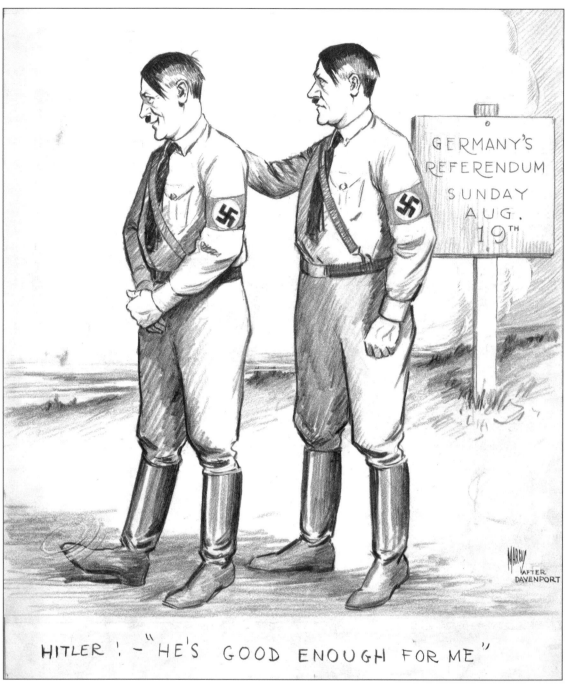

By permission of the Marcus family

"He's Good Enough for Me" by Edwin Marcus (1934): This image is based on the most famous pro-Roosevelt cartoons produced in 1904 and 1912 by Homer Davenport, where Uncle Sam endorses Teddy Roosevelt. This time Hitler is recommending a clone of himself as president of Germany. When Hindenburg died in 1934, Hitler announced that his position of chancellor would merge with the presidency and that he would then be the *Fuehrer*. In a plebiscite, this arrangement was approved by 90 percent of voters, or that's how it was announced. (Believe that, and you'll believe anything!)

"Zero Hour" by François (1935): Hitler prepares to decapitate a kneeling Europe, whose attempts to appease him (symbolized by the olive branch held in a cuffed hand) have failed, as a bloody stain spreads out across the continent. The Treaties of Versailles and Locarno lie torn up on the ground. This cartoon could refer to the plebiscite in the Free City of Danzig, which went to the Nazis and was seen as the spark to ignite war.

STILL MORE FRATERNISATION.

MR. PUNCH (*preparing for a trip to Salzburg, after learning that all Austrian Nazis are compelled to grow* HITLER *moustaches*)—

"AND I DO HOPE THEY WON'T NOTICE THE NOSE."

"Still More Fraternisation" by E. H. Shepard (1935): Rumors that Austrian Nazis had to grow Hitler moustaches en masse prompted this cartoon in *Punch*.

LEFT: "Their Agreement" (1934): Caricature from a Romanian leftist magazine in which Goering is saying: "Don't you agree there are too many agreements being signed in Europe?" Goebbels replies: "It doesn't matter, because we won't stick to any of them."

BELOW: "The New Lilliput" by Derso and Kelen (1938): Adolf Hitler luxuriates in his power over the diplomats of Europe at the Munich Conference, where France and Britain agreed to allow Germany to annex the Sudetenland as long as Hitler promised not to invade anywhere else. (Fat chance!) In the bottom right-hand corner, Lord Halifax is bragging to Chamberlain: "Don't be afraid. I know him personally… he's a vegetarian." Emery Kelen and Alois Derso were Hungarian Jews who worked for the League of Nations in Geneva in the 1920s and 1930s, and quit Europe for the USA in 1938 on the eve of war.

THE NEW LILLIPUT

Lord Halifax to Chamberlain: "Don't be afraid, I know him personally … He is a vegetarian!"

STEPPING STONES TO GLORY.

"Stepping Stones to Glory" by David Low (1936): In this anti-appeasement cartoon, Hitler goose-steps across a red carpet laid out on the backs of the "spineless leaders of democracy" as he marches toward his goal as "Boss of the Universe." The way Low drew Hitler really got under the *Fuehrer*'s skin, so much so that the Nazis put pressure on the British government in 1937 for Low to rein it in. He was asked to stop drawing Hitler because it was thought he might provoke the Germans into doing something rash (like invading other countries). The London *Evening Standard*, Low's employer, was banned in Germany too! Low responded to the ban with a new character called Muzzler, a composite Mussolini-Hitler dictator stereotype. Once Germany took over Austria in 1938 and Germany's aggressive intentions were there for all to see, the gloves were off and Low was free to mock Hitler as much as he liked. He renewed the attack with relish.

THANKS TO FASCISM—1936 !

Will Dyson, *Daily Herald*, 23.12.1936, the British Cartoon Archive, University of Kent, www.cartoons.ac.uk

"Thanks to Fascism—1936!" by Will Dyson (1936): Dyson shows things heating up in the "arms pit" as the world falls into the grip of fascism while the Devil watches on approvingly. In 1936, Oswald Mosley led his Blackshirts through London's East End to provoke the area's large Jewish population. This led to the Battle of Cable Street, where the Metropolitan Police tried to keep control as the British Union of Fascists took on assorted socialists, trade unionists, anarchists, Irish groups and Jews. Around 175 people were hospitalized, and the ringleaders were sentenced to three months' hard labor.

ST ADOLF PREACHES TO THE BIRDS

(HUMBLY SUBMITTED BY MR. PUNCH AS A 100% ARYAN PICTURE SUITABLE FOR HANGING IN ANY GERMAN ART GALLERY.)

Right: "*La Cagoule*" by Raoul Cabrol (1938): The *Cagoulards*, so called after the hoods they wore, were clandestine right-wing terrorists active in France in the 1930s, many of whom became Nazi collaborators.

Opposite: "St. Adolf Preaches to the Birds" by E. H. Shepard (1937): The beauty of this cartoon is that it follows the rules of Nazi art and mocks them at the same time. The *Haus der Deutschen Kunst* in Munich exclusively featured "approved Nazi art"—mostly peasant idylls, idealized portraits of German workers, neoclassical nudes in pseudo-Hellenic settings, and heroic military missions expressing love and longing for the Homeland.

Below: "The 'Big Noise' for Peace" by Don Angus (1938): The Munich Agreement of 1938, attended by most of Europe's major powers (bar Russia), permitted Germany to annex parts of Czechoslovakia, a country which was not invited to discussions. Chamberlain called it "peace in our time," but it was more like abject appeasement.

THE "BIG NOISE" FOR PEACE?

THE STATUE OF FREIHEIT?

"Our ideal cannot be held within bounds. It has submerged Germany beneath its wave, and who can be surprised if it is now spreading beyond our frontiers, everywhere Germans live?"—*Herr Hitler speaking in Berlin.*

ABOVE: "The Statue of Freiheit?" by Bernard Partridge (1938): Designed to bring home to Americans the threat of the Nazis after Hitler's Berlin speech, this cartoon imagines potential Nazi amendments to the Statue of Liberty. Sure enough, it would be alarming to wake up and see this on Staten Island.

OPPOSITE: "The Aryan Ark" by Bernard Partridge (1938): This too was designed to let the US know about Germany's vaulting ambition. Before the war the Nazis had planned to set up colonies in South America. This cartoon features a particularly enjoyable version of Goebbels as a simpering wooden toy.

THE ARYAN ARK

Herr Hitler (to the Bird of Peace). " Get along and find me some colonies."

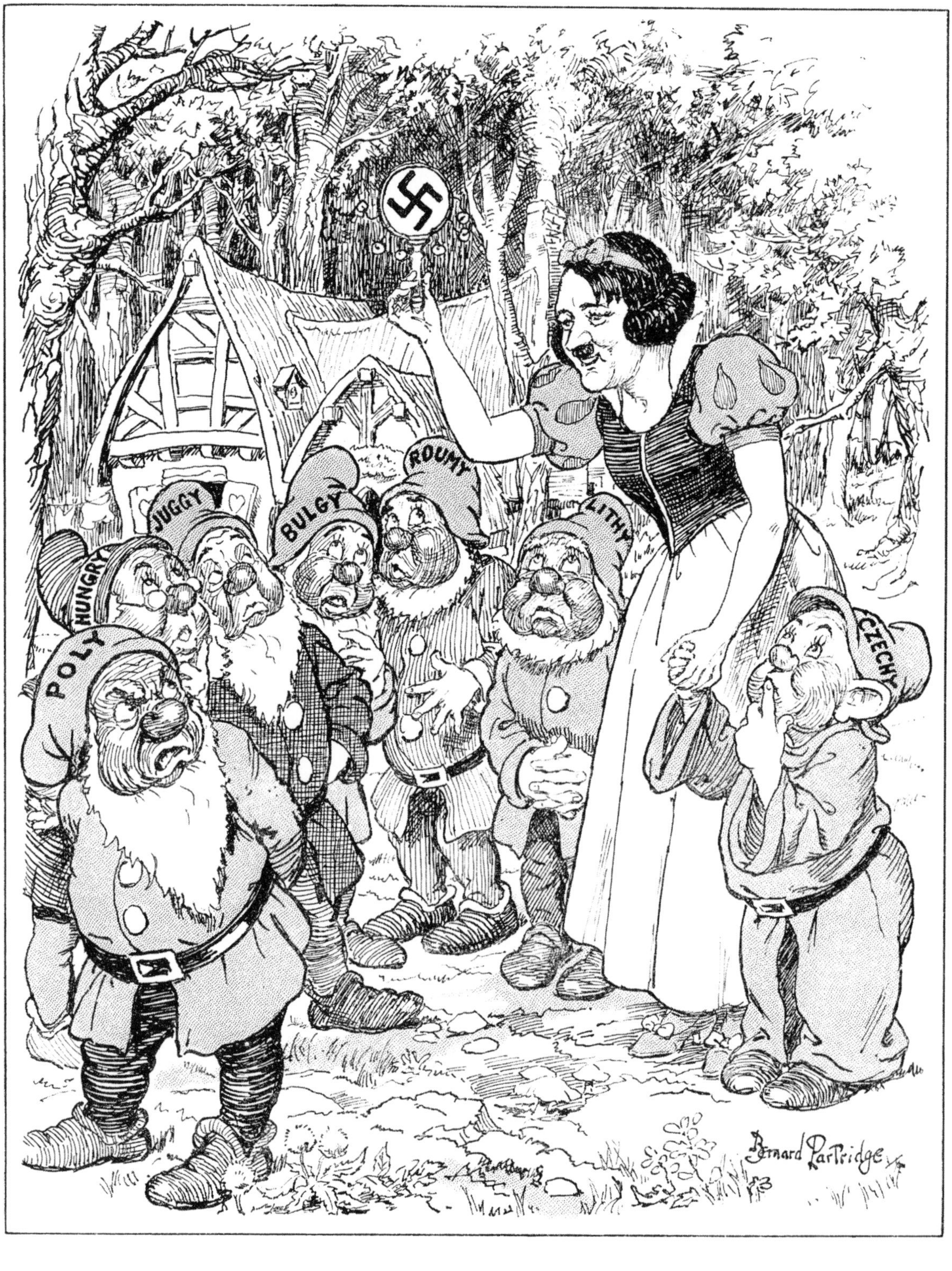
ROUMY
BULGY
JUGGY
LITHY
HUNGRY
POLY
CZECHY
Bernard Partridge

—— —— AND THE SEVEN DWARFS

DESIGN FOR PEACE

"Design for Peace" by Gordon Minhinnick (1939): Hitler sports angel wings but that's only for show; it's his gun and cat-o'-nine-tails you have to watch out for. (In other words, don't believe his offer of peace.) Minhinnick was born in Cornwall, England, and emigrated to New Zealand, where he ended up working for the *New Zealand Herald*. He was a great friend of David Low and was offered Low's job at the London *Evening Standard* when the great man left in 1949. Minhinnick turned the offer down, but readers might not have noticed anything had changed since their styles are so similar.

OPPOSITE: "— — and the Seven Dwarfs" by Bernard Partridge (1938): In 1937 Walt Disney's film *Snow White and the Seven Dwarfs* opened to massive critical acclaim and popular success. In this cartoon Bernard Partridge casts Hitler as Snow White, holding aloft a Nazi swastika, while the countries of eastern Europe are the seven dwarfs, who look on and wonder what the future holds for them. Hitler's all-time favorite films were said to be *King Kong* and *Snow White*.

"For you, a nice tin soldier to play with, while we send daddy to General Franco to play with!"
Hitler's Christmas present to his little friends is a toy German soldier, fully equipped.

Will Dyson, *Daily Herald*, 23.12.1936, the British Cartoon Archive, University of Kent, www.cartoons.ac.uk

"For you, a nice tin soldier to play with, while we send daddy to General Franco to play with" by Will Dyson (1936): To save Europe from "communist barbarism" as well as to cement relations with fascist Italy which supported Franco, Hitler sent bombers and fighter planes, as well as 15,000 troops, to Spain before the Non-Intervention Agreement of 1936. Toy soldiers were encouraged by the Nazis. You could get the SA, the SS, the LSSAH (Hitler's personal SS bodyguard), the Hitler Youth, and many other designations. The best-selling toy figures at the time included multiple versions of Hitler, Goering, Hess, Goebbels, Mussolini, and Franco. Many came complete with a movable right arm, which was ideal for performing the Nazi salute. Sadly, the ever-popular Ernst Röhm figure was dropped after the thuggish Nazi streetfighter was executed during the "Night of the Long Knives" and promptly written out of Nazi history.

"See how in four short years I have increased the Might of the Fatherland!"

Will Dyson, *Daily Herald*, 2.2.1937, the British Cartoon Archive, University of Kent, www.cartoons.ac.uk

"See how in four short years I have increased the Might of the Fatherland!" by Will Dyson (1937): Dyson's satire on the futility of building up your military forces because your enemy is duty bound to follow suit. Germany looks outnumbered here, but of course when Russia became Germany's ally early in the war, the balance looked as if it had tipped in the Nazis' favor.

"Take me to Czechoslovakia, Driver" by Vaughn Shoemaker (1938): Hermann Goering called this cartoon from the *Chicago Times* "a horrible example of anti-Nazi propaganda." Having taken over Austria without a shot being fired (*Anschluss*), Hitler now wanted the Sudetenland, the German-speaking region of Czechoslovakia.

ABOVE: "The Blitzkrieg in France and Denmark" (1940): This appeared in *Signal*, a glossy propaganda sheet published fortnightly by the German *Wehrmacht* in 30 different languages. At its height it had a circulation of 2.5 million. You couldn't buy it in Germany, but it was widely available in the US until December 1941.

ABOVE: "The Possible Successor at the Photographer's" by Jenny Goldberg (1940s): The Fregoli delusion is a rare disorder where an individual believes that a number of different people are the same person in disguise. Perhaps inspired by Goering's habit of changing his clothes three or four times a day, this pokes fun at his vanity and ambition to succeed the *Fuehrer*.

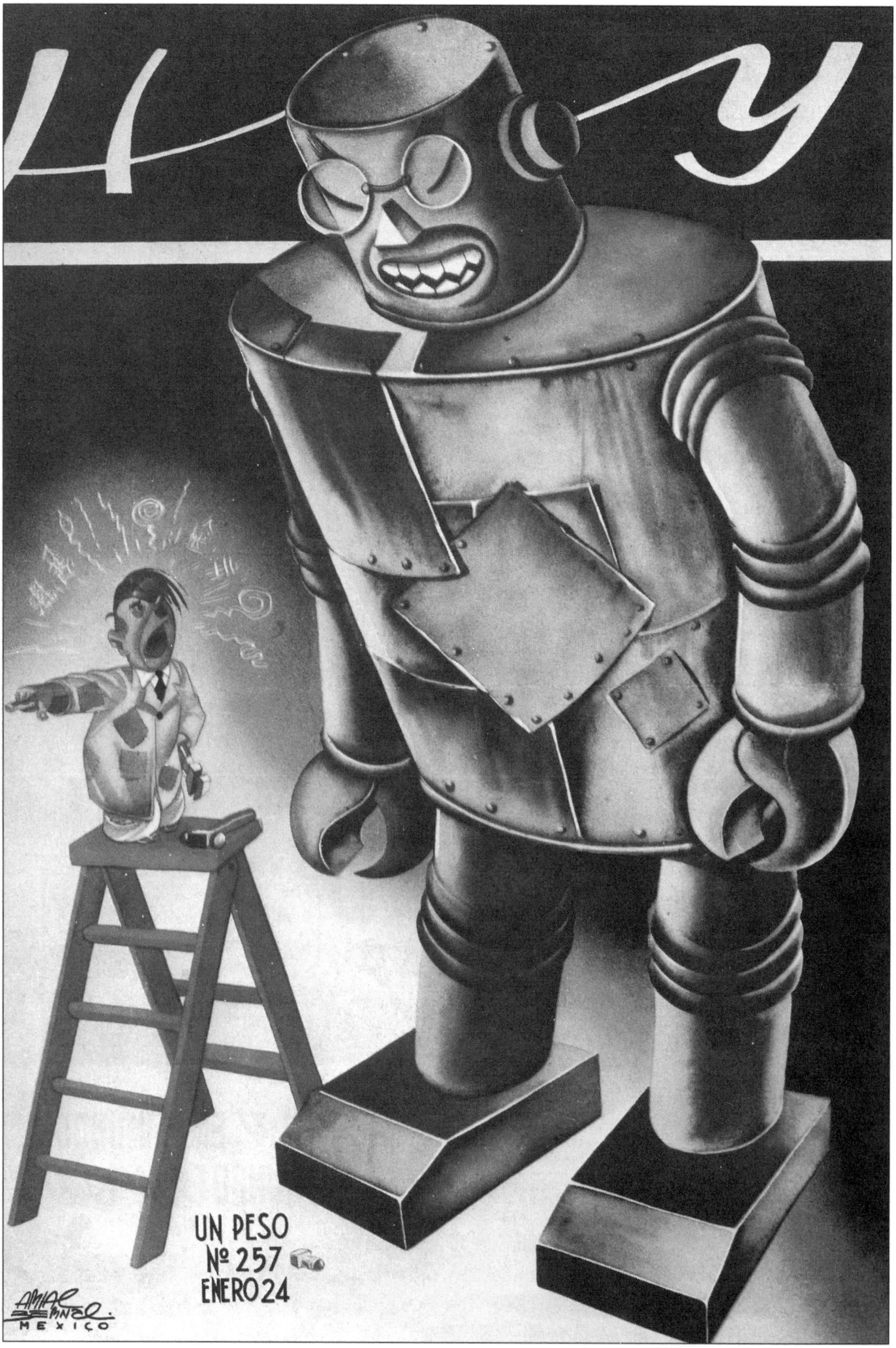
Hoy
UN PESO
Nº 257
ENERO 24
MEXICO

SOMEONE IS TAKING SOMEONE FOR A WALK

Opposite: After a few quick repairs, Hitler orders the Japanese war robot into action in this cartoon by Antonio Arias Bernal (1939). This was the cover of Mexican weekly *Hoy* ("Today"). Bernal was an anti-Axis cartoonist. Known as "The Brigadier," he worked for the US government during the war. The *New York Times* named him "The Top Cartoonist of WWII" and he also worked for *Life* and *Colliers Magazine*.

"Someone is Taking Someone for a Walk" by David Low (1939): Low didn't think there was much to choose between Stalin and Hitler after the deal they had done (which included oil supplies). During review sessions of the foreign press, Hitler would explode with rage whenever he saw Low's work, which was exactly what the cartoonist had set out to achieve. Low was said to be high on the Nazis' death list, to be implemented as soon as Britain had been invaded.

THE MINOTAUR

Above: "The Minotaur" by E. H. Shepard (1941): This cartoon appeared during the Blitz. It's based on a painting by George Frederic Watts. The Minotaur, half-man, half-bull, could only be placated by human sacrifice.

Opposite: "Under Two Flags" by Edwin Marcus (1939): The gorilla of aggression sallies forth under the swastika <u>and</u> the hammer & sickle. (The title came from a popular 19th-century novel.) Germany and the Soviet Union signed their non-aggression pact in August 1939 as Germany invaded Poland, and the Soviet Union moved into Finland, prompting this cartoon.

AGGRESSION

UNDER TWO FLAGS

By permission of the Marcus family

TRIPARTITE PACT

" Hear no good ! "   " See no good ! "   " Speak no good ! "

"Tripartite Pact" by Bernard Partridge (1940): One of the most popular brass ornaments of the 1940s was the Three Wise Monkeys which would sit quietly on your mantelpiece, hearing no evil, seeing no evil, speaking no evil—in fact turning away from anything that might prove in any way upsetting. This was Bernard Partridge's entertaining inversion, featuring Japan, Germany, and Italy.

JEKYLL AND HYDE

"Jekyll and Hyde" by Bernard Partridge (1940): Hitler goes from smarmy nice guy to lurching, frenzied monster after drinking a potion marked "Lust of power." Robert Louis Stevenson's novel *Jekyll and Hyde* offered insight into the duality of human beings, but there could have been other explanations for Hitler's behavior. It's thought he suffered from chronic flatulence and regularly took 74 different medications, including methamphetamine.

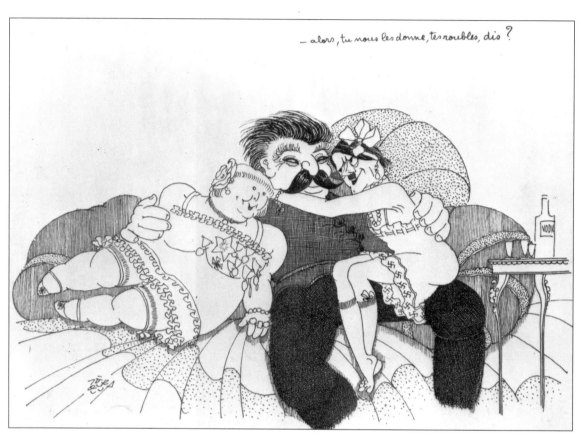

"– alors, tu nous les donne, tes roubles, dis ?"

"*Alors, tu nous les donnes, tes roubles, dis?*":
Drab *ménage à trois*, featuring Stalin and
two money-grabbing prostitutes who
look uncannily like Goering and Hitler.
"Don't forget to hand over your roubles,"
they remind their client. Interesting
details include the row of medals on
Goering's night-dress and the swastikas
on Hitler's slip. Stalin's big sausage
fingers are rather disconcerting, though,
as he curls them around his floozies.

OPPOSITE: "Fifth Horseman of the Apocalypse" by D. R. Fitzpatrick
(1940): In 1940 the German air force was riding high, having
played a large part in conquering Poland and in victories across
Europe. Hermann Goering was a national hero, but this was
about to change after the Battle of Britain and other setbacks,
which proved what an incompetent air force leader he really was.

FIFTH HORSEMAN OF THE APOCALYPSE.

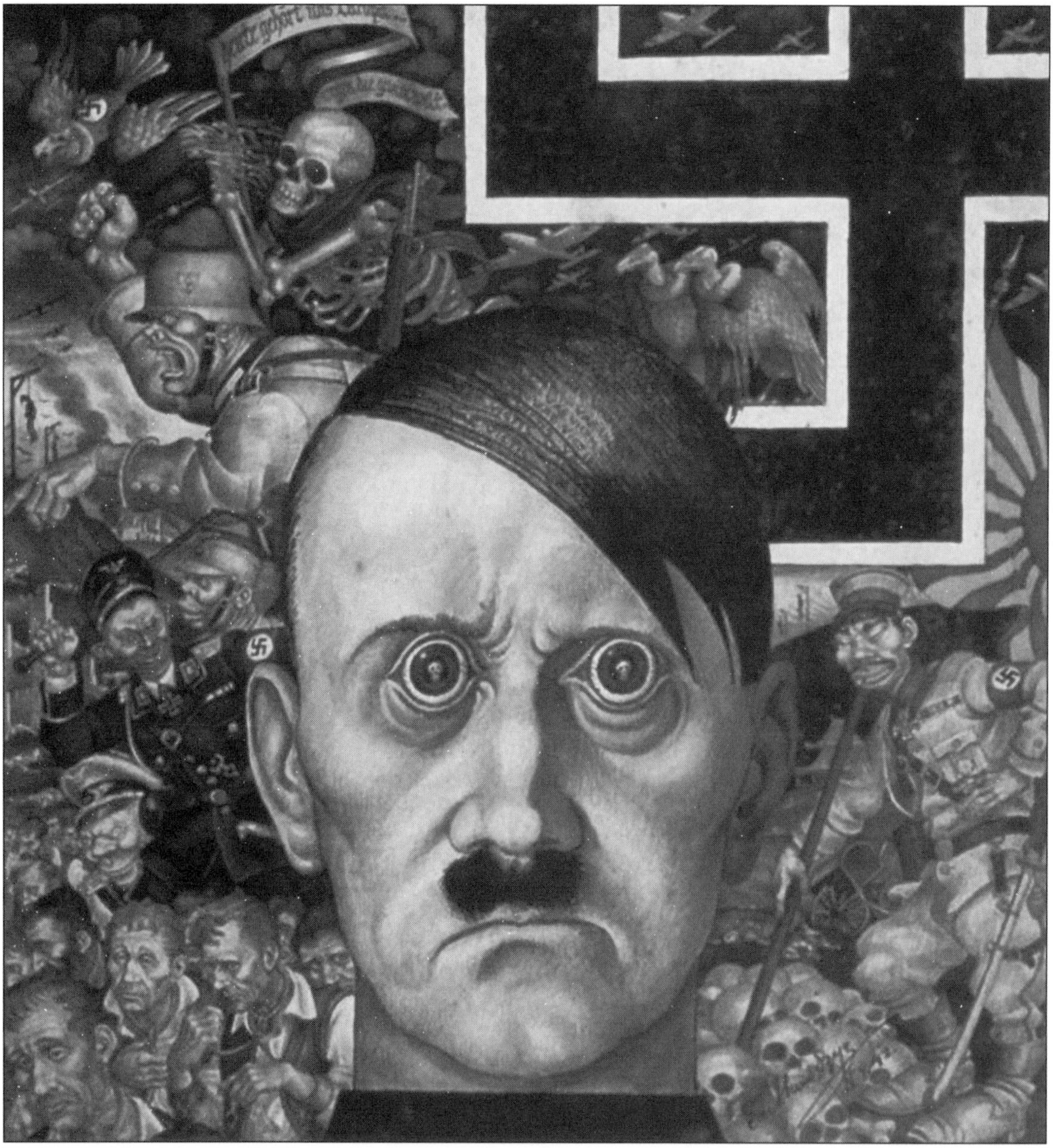

"The Anti-Christ" by Arthur Szyk (1942): Polish-Jewish artist Szyk's image, with skulls reflected in the eyes and the words *Vae Victis* (Latin for "woe to the conquered") ingrained in his jet-black comb-over, shows Hitler as the personification of evil. This detailed watercolor and gouache painting overflows with the sheer horror of war: Nazi soldiers, men in manacles, a field of skulls, and a skeleton with a banner featuring a line from a National Socialist song: "*heute gehört uns Deutschland / morgen die ganze Welt*" ["today Germany is ours, tomorrow the whole world"]. This is one of the most chilling images of Hitler by perhaps the greatest anti-Nazi artist.

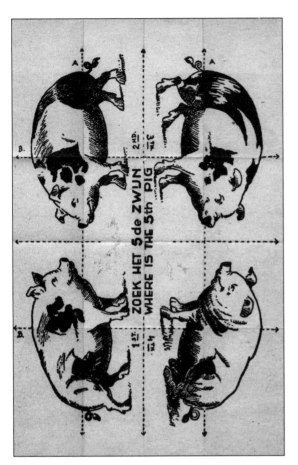

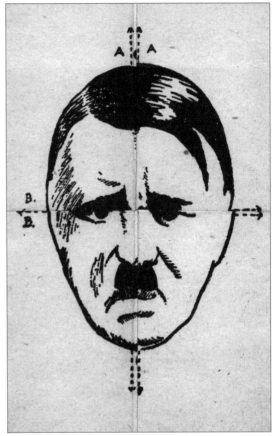

A pleasingly rebellious puzzle from Nazi-occupied Holland in 1942, but the kind of item that could have cost its owner his or her life if the Germans were to find it. The question, "Where is the 5th pig?," is answered by making the correct folds in the picture of the four pigs to create the image above right.

"Are WE Frankensteins?" by Clifford Berryman (1940): Mussolini and Stalin look on in consternation as the German war machine death monster and out-of-control weather system, which they may have given birth to, rumbles into life in alarming studded boots. Will it turn on its creators?

OPPOSITE: *Struwwelhitler* by Robert and Philip Spence (1941): The front cover of a book written in parody of *Struwwelpeter* ("Shock-headed Peter"), the great German collection of cautionary tales for children compiled with such sadistic relish. Here, the inside pages featured Mussolini, Goebbels, and all the other familiar favorites.

Struwwelhitler

A Nazi Story Book
by Doktor Schrecklichkeit

DRAWN FOR
PHILCO
BY
SHERMAN
COOKE

Time is Short, Adolph!

Brilliant US propaganda poster (1942) drawn by Sherman Cooke and sponsored by Philco, who made batteries, radios, and electrical goods: Hitler is up to his knuckles in the world's blood, but his time is running out fast. Posters were everywhere in the US after Pearl Harbor and they were useful for keeping company names in the public eye. Coca-Cola sponsored posters showing defense workers and the armed forces downing its fizzy concoction. Lucky Strike cigarettes claimed to have changed the color of its packaging in order to save bronze for weapons. During the war, commercial companies made big bucks by wrapping themselves in the flag.

OPPOSITE: "The Super-Bully" by Bernard Partridge (1942): Hitler is in characteristic pose with his hands clasped in front of him rather defensively, while he contemplates his all-conquering creation, the super-bully. Meanwhile, the quote below the image seems to echo Wellington's words about the Black Watch on the eve of the battle of Waterloo.

THE SUPER-BULLY

"I don't know if this will frighten the enemy's armies, but it ought to frighten mine."

[The forces of the Nazi Party Corps are to be strengthened, not only for fighting but also for police work throughout the occupied countries and Germany itself.]

IMPROVING THE RACE
Selected breed of delegates for Nazi Congress
Cartoon by Yefimov, 1941

FIB-DETECTORS
German Command's Report of Military Operations
Cartoon by Kukryniksy, 1941

ARABIAN TALES
Cartoon by Kukryniksy, 1941

THE NAZI KENNEL
Cartoon by Kukryniksy, 1941

НАГЛЯДНОЕ ИЗО

БЕЛОКУР

КАК ГИТЛ

TRANSLATION PICTORIA

According to

BLOND LIKE HITLER

The image top left is by Boris Yefimov; the others are all by Kukryniksy. Kukryniksy was the name adopted by three Russian caricaturists, Mikhail Kupryanov, Porfirii Krylov, and Nikolai Sokolov, who met at art school in Moscow in the 1920s. They learned how to apply their keen sense of the grotesque to political subjects and became rising stars of Soviet publications such as *Krokodil* and *Pravda*. During World War II, they produced over 70 propaganda posters for the TASS studio in Moscow and after the war they were sent to document the Nuremberg trials by *Pravda*. They were renowned for their poison-pen portraits of Hitler, Mussolini, Franco, and other fascist dictators.

"Leaders of the Master Race" by Boris Yefimov (1941): A poster designed for international distribution. Yefimov was one of the great anti-Nazi cartoonists. David Low described him as "an artist of the comic, specializing in the destructive power of ridicule." The son of a Jewish shoemaker born in Kiev, he lived through dangerous times. His brother was executed by Stalin, but he was spared because he was needed for the propaganda war. Yefimov lived to 109, old enough to have seen the last czar pass by in a coach, to have known Trotsky, and to vote for Putin.

"The Neighborhood Watch Dog" by Jay "Ding" Darling (1941): Two burglars, Hitler and Mussolini, step right across a bad-tempered sleeping dog with Josef Stalin's face into a house labeled "Back Door of Europe." A worried couple, representing Greece and Turkey, watch from the window as the dictators enter their premises with the clear intention of robbing them blind.

"Caught In His Own Bear Trap" by Jay "Ding" Darling (1942): Hitler is caught rather painfully in a huge bear trap attached to a stanchion labeled "Stalingrad." A Russian bear fires a gun at him while two small bears jump up and down in glee. Most historians agree that Hitler's failure to capture Stalingrad, and the subsequent Soviet encirclement and defeat of his armies there in the winter of 1942/3, marked the turning point of World War II.

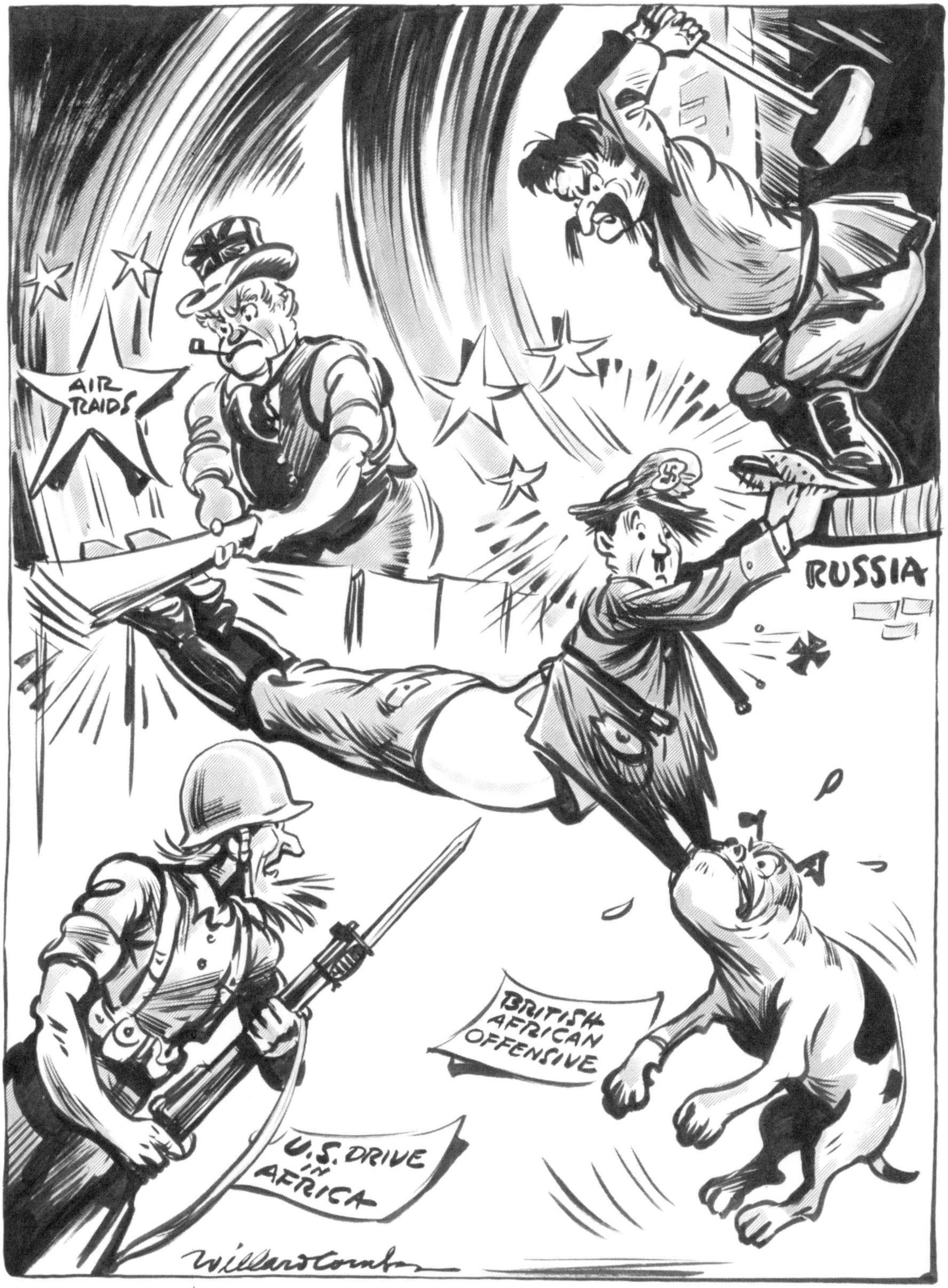
AIR RAIDS
RUSSIA
BRITISH AFRICAN OFFENSIVE
U.S. DRIVE IN AFRICA
Willard Combes

Right: Excerpts from the cover of Mexican anti-fascist magazine, *El Ejie* (1942). One shows Benito Juárez, symbol of Mexican democracy, pointing a crowd of Nazis toward the Hill of Bells (where a firing squad killed Archduke Ferdinand Maximilian in 1867—the Austrian was installed as Emperor of Mexico by Napoleon III in 1864). The second has Stalin and Hitler in a Turkish bath; Hitler is being told his massage is about to begin.

Opposite: "Over Extended" by Willard Combes (1942): This cartoon published in the *Cleveland Press* pretty much sums up the situation of Hitler in 1942, with Stalin hammering him on the head and standing on his fingers; John Bull bombing the hell out of German cities; and Uncle Sam and the British Bulldog hounding his forces out of North Africa. Combes further mocked the superstitious *Fuehrer* with this caption: "Consult your nearest astrologer, Adolf! What do the stars say, Adolf?"

Below: "You're slipping, Doctor Goebbels" by the Office for Emergency Management, War Production Board (1943): Hitler is demanding reassurance from his Minister of Propaganda. This was another wartime cartoon sponsored by Philco.

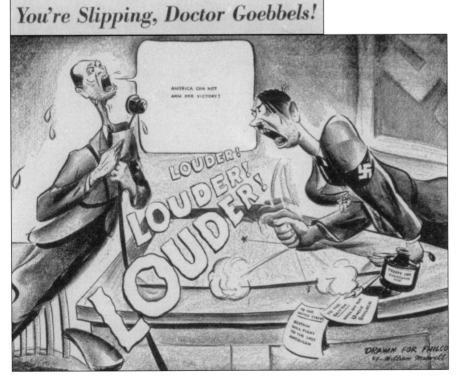

"Transformation of the Krauts" by Kukryniksy (1943): A brilliant cartoon which succinctly tells the story of the German invasion of the USSR. The Axis Powers lost some 850,000 men, killed, wounded and captured, at Stalingrad. It was perhaps the grimmest battle of all time, with some 1.7 million to 2 million casualties on both the Axis and Soviet sides.

OPPOSITE: "They Can't Scare Him—Much" by Clifford Berryman (1943): Hitler goose-steps quickly past a graveyard clutching his speech. His dream of world conquest has been laid to rest and he's haunted by Stalin, Roosevelt, and Churchill. After Italy surrendered to the Allies in September 1943, Hitler made a speech about how the Allies would never pierce the "ring of steel" around the German Empire, a far cry from his original ambition of world domination.

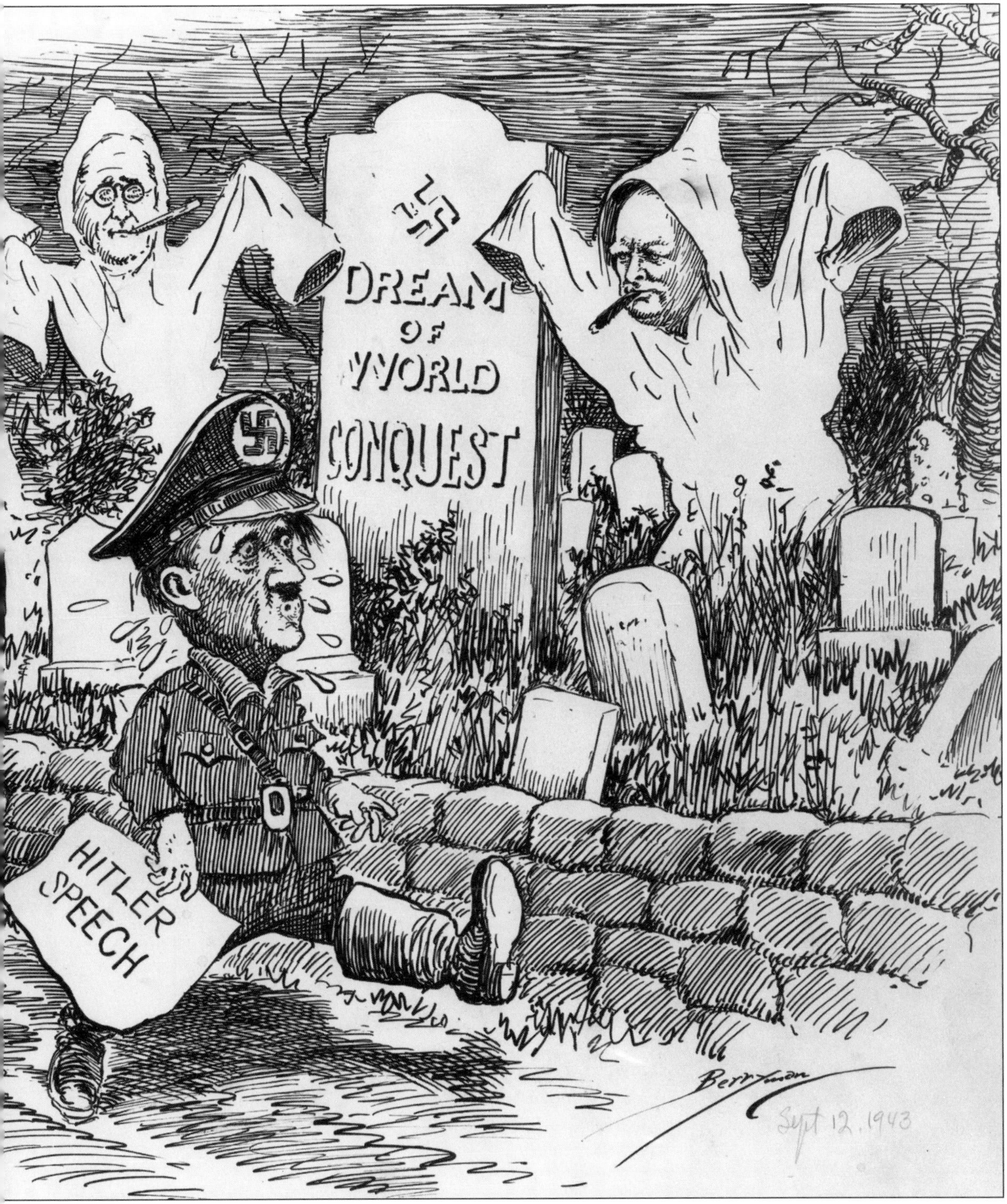
DREAM OF WORLD CONQUEST
HITLER SPEECH
Berryman
Sept 12, 1943

Kukryniksy cartoon that shows Hitler, Goering and Himmler as strutting cockerels looking across the Channel to England, and saying "Where will we land?" (1940); by 1943, they are mangy, soaked and bedraggled, and the question has changed to "Where will <u>they</u> land?" Some Russian cartoonists had very cruel imaginations!

HIS SERVANT'S VOICE

"His Servant's Voice" by Illingworth (1945): Leslie Illingworth's brilliant drawing of Hitler as Himmler's puppet was designed to reinforce the rumor that Himmler had taken over the reins in Germany, Hitler being a spent force. In reality, Hitler might have been doomed, but he was still barking out orders.

"Do You Want Total War?" by Herbert Marxen (c.1945): "*Wollt ihr den Totalen Krieg*" echoes the words of Josef Goebbels in a speech given to a carefully chosen audience by the German Propaganda Minister at Berlin Sportpalast in February 1943 after the tide of war had turned against the Axis Powers. It was the first time the Nazis ever admitted to facing difficulties in the war. Dominating the hall was a massive banner that read, '*TOTALER KRIEG—KÜRZESTER KRIEG*', meaning "total war, shortest war." Marxen was one of the leading anti-Nazi artists in post-war Germany.

OPPOSITE: Hitler and Mussolini work diligently, in this image from 1945, to try to patch up their puppet soldier who has been mangled and shot to pieces, and dragged through a hedge backward by war—even his pegleg is broken in two. Hitler is sewing his sleeve back on, Musso is nailing his forearm back in place, but you can't help feeling the damage is well beyond repair. A case of too little too late.

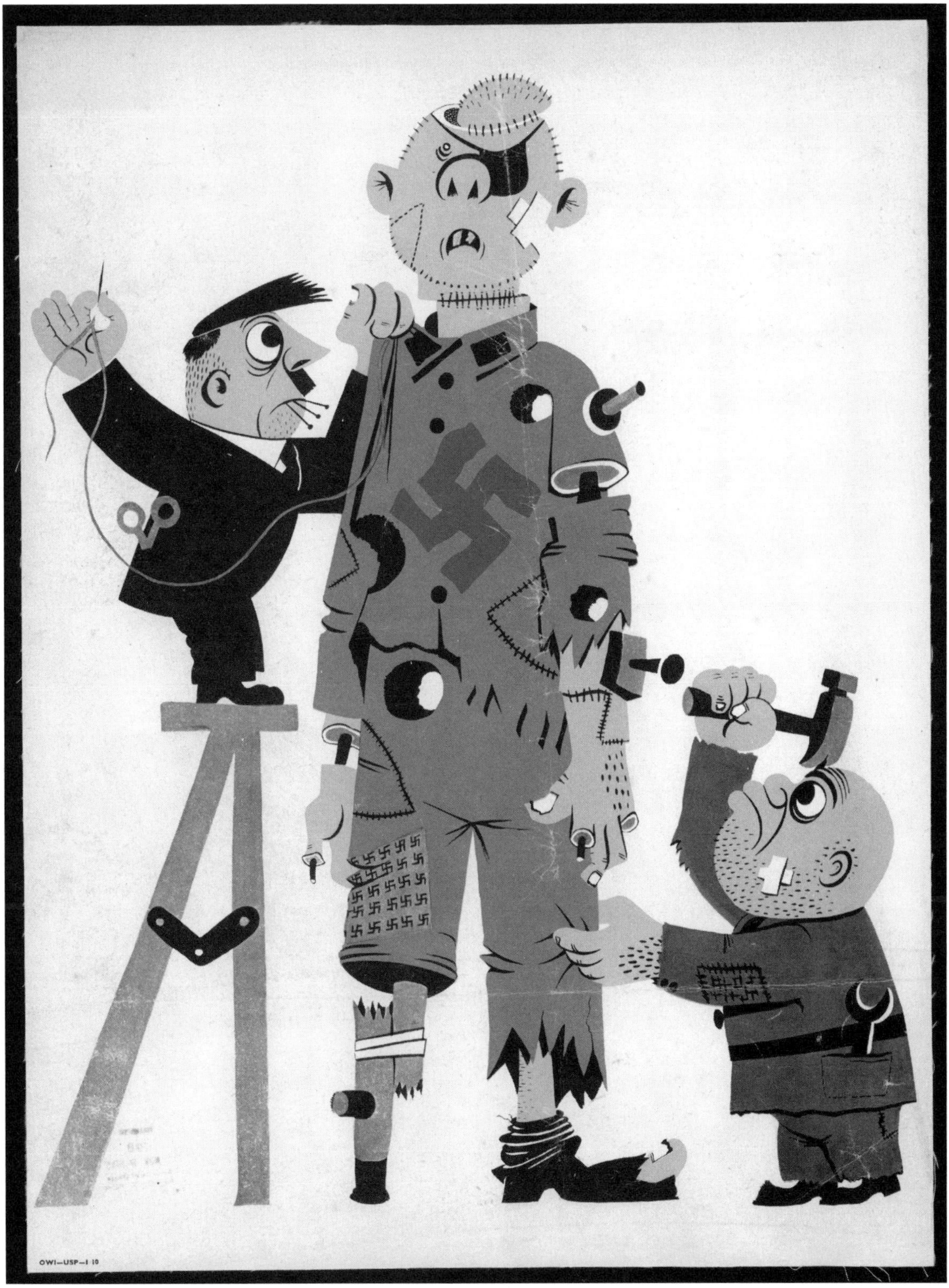
OWI—USP—I 10

Spanish Serenade!

"Spanish Serenade" by Philip Zec (1940): This cartoon was drawn following a meeting
between Hitler and Franco at Hendaye on the Spanish–French border. Hitler tried
everything he could to persuade Franco to invade the British overseas territory of Gibraltar.

Chapter 5

FRANCO
El Generalísimo

Franco was not the most flamboyant of dictators; in fact he was rather austere. He liked to appear in public in military uniform exuding a strong sense of duty. If he could be pictured next to another dictator, then that was all to the good. Cartoonists picked up on his apparent inertia by tending to draw him among his peer group of dictators as the little guy being told what to do. He did not lack detractors. One of them was the great artist Pablo Picasso, who drew a series of posh cartoons called "The Dream and the Lie of Franco" (1937), sending up the idea that he had ever done anything for Spain or for its culture. Nonetheless Franco was in power from 1939 until his death in 1975, a pretty long innings for a dictator.

"The Spanish See-Saw" by Bernard Partridge (1936): This cartoon lampoons British Foreign Secretary Anthony Eden's policy of non-intervention in the Spanish Civil War. He stands there bemused as the see-saw goes up and down. On the left (the right, politically) is Franco supported by Hitler and Mussolini; on the right, is Caballero supported by Stalin and France's premier Blum. Caballero was prime minister of the Second Spanish Republic during the Civil War. Blum was the first Socialist premier of France, presiding over the Popular Front coalition, 1936–7.

THI

MR. EDEN. "THIS MAY BE A NEW 'BALANCE

SPANISH SEE-SAW

"F POWER,' BUT IT CERTAINLY ISN'T 'COLLECTIVE SECURITY.'"

THE DUMMY THAT SPOKE BY ITSELF

ADOLF } (together). "WHERE DID THAT ONE COME FROM—YOU OR ME?"
BENITO }

"The Franco Composite Aircraft" by E. H. Shepard (1937): This monstrous concoction was the invention of E. H. Shepard (who famously also illustrated A. A. Milne's *Winnie the Pooh*). Italy sent Franco 50 fighters and 12 reconnaissance planes. Spain was also used as the testing ground for Germany's WWII bombing tactics, a campaign they began against the Basques in March 1937. April 26 was the date of the bombing of Guernica, which featured 23 Junkers Ju52 bombers among a total of 80 German planes. Later, Junkers Ju52s terror-bombed Durango, killing 248 people.

THE FRANCO COMPOSITE AIRCRAFT

The Upper Component. "THANKS FOR THE LIFT, BUT I'M SURE YOU'LL AGREE THAT I CAN MANAGE NOW WITHOUT YOUR SUPPORT."

OPPOSITE: "The Dummy That Spoke By Itself" by Bernard Partridge (1937): Hitler and Mussolini try to blame each other for the words their "puppet" Franco is coming out with, since both dictators were all for sending more troops to Spain. Mussolini, who considered himself a brilliant military commander at this stage, was constantly critical of the way Franco ran his campaign during the Spanish Civil War; this turned out to be a case of the pot calling the kettle black once the serious business of WWII began and his own deficiences were revealed.

VICTIMS of ANOTHER FILM HOLD-UP

Will Dyson, *Daily Herald*, 1.4.1937, the British Cartoon Archive, University of Kent, www.cartoons.ac.uk

"Victims of Another Film Hold-up" by Will Dyson (1937): Hitler and Mussolini look distinctly fed up. They've been upstaged by Franco who's playing the lead in a major drama, the Spanish Civil War, which has not been progressing as it should. Filming has come to a halt. Our two glum dictators feel they've been stitched up after all the time and money they've put into the production.

"All are Gone, the Old Familiar Fasces" by Herb Block (1962): Aged Franco sits in his decrepit castle, a vulture perched on the back of his chair, surrounded by portraits of Hitler, Mussolini, and Trujillo Molina, dictator of the Dominican Republic who was assassinated in 1961. Ex-criminal Molina specialized in torture, murder, and spending his people's money. He once said, "He who does not know how to deceive does not know how to rule."

"The New Religion" by Ed Valtman (1966): A huge, Buddha-like figure is borne aloft by brainwashed followers mindlessly chanting words from *The Little Red Book*. Many Western commentators praised China's Cultural Revolution, but Valtman, a refugee from Soviet rule in Estonia, understood the cult of personality only too well.

Chapter 6

MAO Zedong

The rules for producing images of Mao Zedong were really quite strict. You couldn't use any old colors; they had to be "hong, guang, liang" —red, bright and shining. Similarly you could only show him as an inspiring figure, such as the benevolent father, the wise statesman, the military leader or the great teacher. It was best too that he was also the source of light in any painting, so the faces of those surrounding him could be lit up by what he was saying. Mao insisted on being seen as a godlike figure from whom all good things emanated. But, sadly, the harsh punishments that resulted from unsatisfactory depictions of Mao didn't leave Chinese cartoonists much room. That's why all the images in this section had to come from elsewhere.

CHINESE COMPOSITION

The Master said: "Artful speech and an ingratiating demeanour rarely accompany virtue."
Analect of Confucius

"Chinese Composition" by Illingworth (1953): This commemorates the signing of the Armistice in Korea and the Independence of Laos from French rule. Back in 1953 China was an implacable enemy of the US as Mao Zedong preached an increasingly radical revolutionary ideology, which embraced the paradox of "using war to promote peace." Here, Mao releases a dove from his left hand and an eagle from his right. He was hard to read.

"Vicky's Willow-Pattern Plate" by Vicky (1954): A Geneva conference was set up to settle issues surrounding the Korean peninsula and Indo-China. Around the table were the Soviet Union, France, UK, US, and China, which meant a split between East and West. The Battle of Dien Bien Phu recommenced on March 13, 1954 during the conference. Eventually the Viet Minh defeated the French, which led to the French signing the Geneva Accords in July 1954, ending their presence in Indo-China. Enter the USA…

"He might be less of a nuisance if we put him on the Board."

[Red China's membership of the UN has been proposed, and rejected, at every session since January 1950]

Ed Valtman's portrait (probably from the 1960s) of Mao is restrained, but he almost certainly did not intend it to be flattering (see also page 148). There's something about the way Mao is clapping that suggests how mighty a dictator he is—he knows his minimal efforts will spark a great outbreak of applause all around China. That's power.

Opposite: "He Might Be Less of a Nuisance If We Put Him on the Board" by Illingworth (1963): Red China's membership of the UN had been proposed, and rejected, at every session since January 1950. The Republic of China (Taiwan) had been a charter member of the United Nations, and one of five permanent members of the UN Security Council, since WWII ended. The People's Republic of China, led by Mao, took its place in 1971.

"Confuse us. He say…" by Emmwood (1958): Mao assumes the pose of the Buddha as the cartoonist nods to Confucius, while Nikita Khrushchev, Charles de Gaulle, Harold Macmillan, and Dwight Eisenhower puzzle over how to deal with China. In 1958, Mao launched his Great Leap Forward, a ruthless economic program, resulting in the Great Chinese Famine and the deaths of 45 million people.

"Who let him in?"

"Who Let Him In?" by Franklin (1969): Naughty Chairman Mao fires his catapult at the dancers during the Russian Folk Dancing Season at the Albert Hall, London. This was a reference to the Sino–Soviet split, which followed a series of armed clashes on the border between China and the Soviet Union.

"Shake on it."

"Shake On It" by Griffin (1991): Some skepticism is expressed here about the
sincerity of Saddam Hussein's offer of their own province to Kurdish refugees on
the Turkey–Iraq border to get them to return home.

Chapter 7

MODERN DESPOTS,
Demagogues and Control Freaks

In the twentieth century, dictators were directly responsible for more than 100 million deaths as a result of the wars which they started, and the political repression they lovingly stirred into being. Recent history has shown no tailing off in the supply of tyrants. In fact, sometimes the world seems to be in a worse state than ever. In Africa, in Asia, in the Middle East, dictators are running wild, and new cutting-edge technology has given them more and more killing power. But perhaps we in the "free world" should not be too smug. As the British humorist Alan Coren once wrote, "Democracy consists of choosing your dictators, after they've told you what you think it is you want to hear."

EYES OF THE WORLD
"Are we never going to get him in a quiet corner?"

Will Dyson, probably for the *Daily Herald*, 1933, the British Cartoon Archive, University of Kent, www.cartoons.ac.uk

"Eyes of the World" by Will Dyson (1933): Bulgarian Georgi Dimitroff was arrested in Berlin and charged with being part of the "conspiracy" to burn down the Reichstag building. During his trial in Leipzig, he conducted his defence brilliantly, turning the tables on his accusers and winning fame across the world.

OPPOSITE: "*L'Homme Enchâiné*" by Bernard Partridge (1941): Marshal Pétain has his own ball and chain with swastika. At the age of 84, this ex-war hero became Chief of State of Vichy France from 1940 to 1944. He replaced the concept of *liberté, egalité, fraternité* with *travail, famille, patrie*. At 95, he died in jail after his death sentence for treason was commuted.

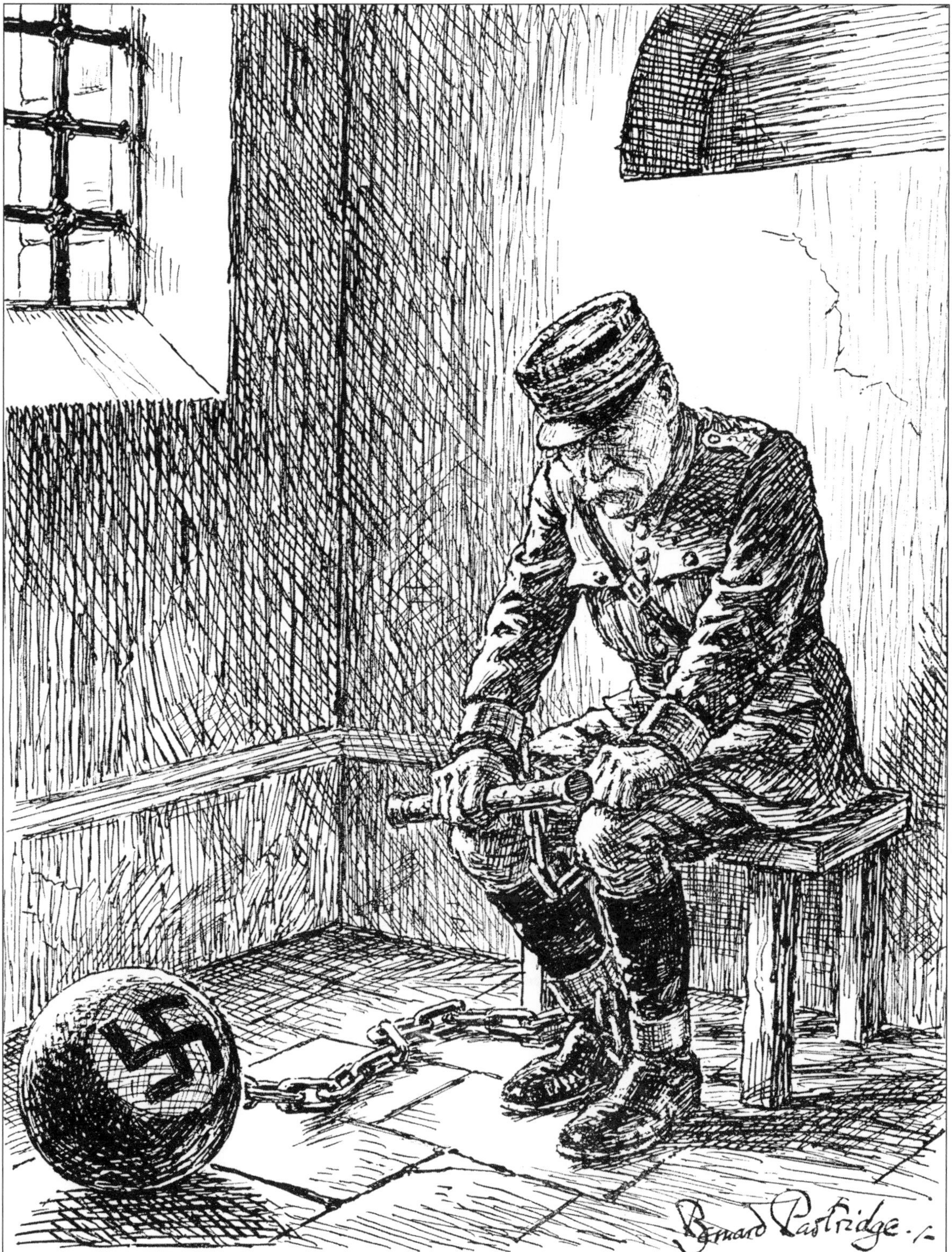
Bernard Partridge

L'HOMME ENCHAÎNÉ

By permission of the Marcus family

"Mickey Mouse" by Edwin Marcus (1949): This cartoon shows
Tito as Mickey Mouse thumbing his nose at a large feline Stalin.
In the late 1940s, Tito refused to accept the domination of Russia
and took an independent line despite Soviet threats. Stalin
wanted a Soviet satellite state, but Tito was having none of it.

"Chiang Kai-shek" (1950): Chiang Kai-shek looks like he's caught between a rock and a hard place in this big handshake between the Soviet Union and China. John Bull and Uncle Sam are trying to free him but only succeed in pulling off his boots. Chiang wasn't the worst dictator ever, but he did have form. For example, the story goes he once had the projectionist thrashed when he didn't like a movie he was being shown. He also initiated the White Terror against dissidents. In the end, the US and the UN stopped recognizing Taiwan and chose to recognize Mao's People's Republic of China instead. That's power politics!

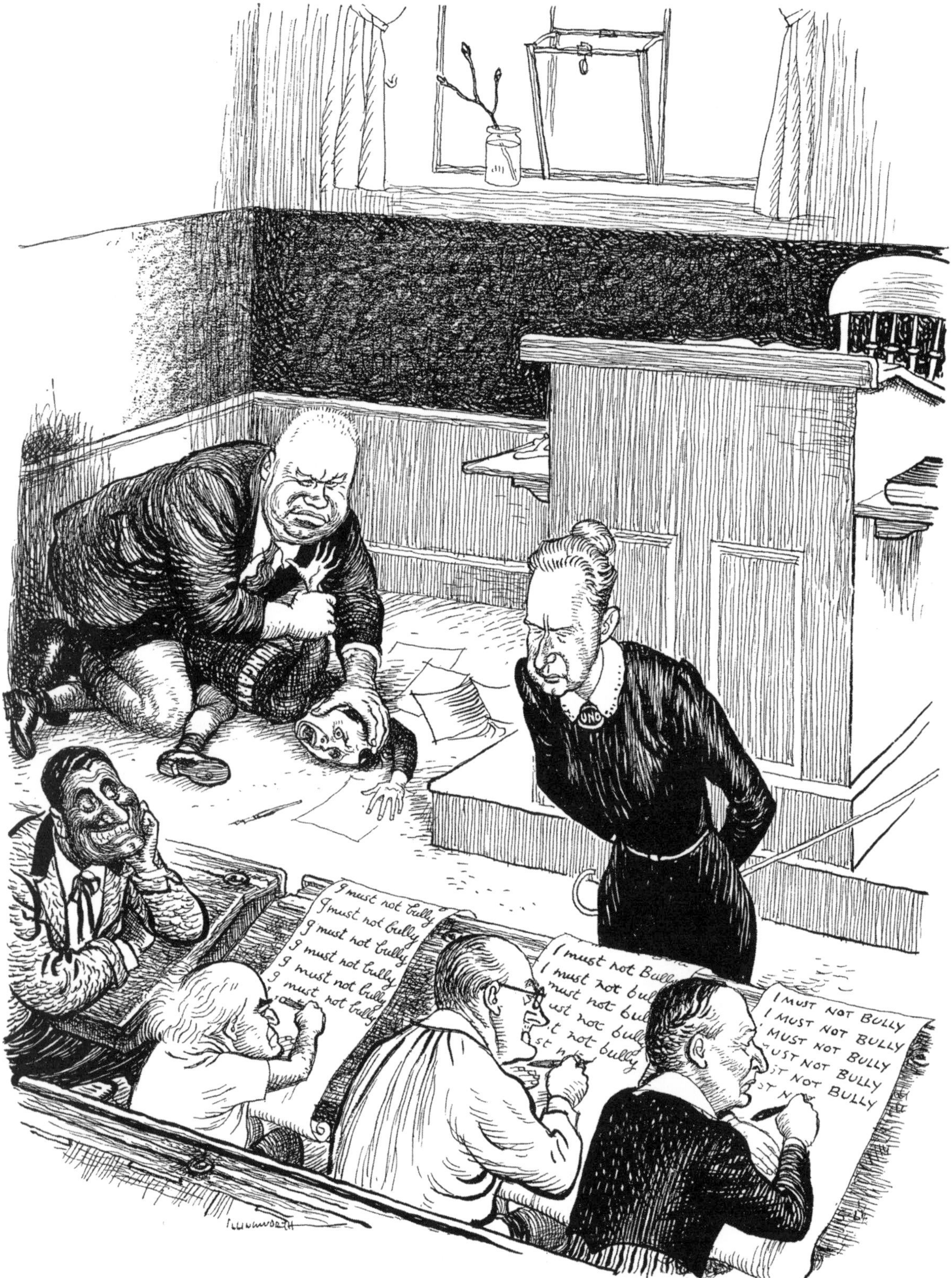
I must not bully
I must not bully
I must not bully
I must not bully
I must not bully
I must not bully
I must not Bully
I must not bully
I MUST NOT BULLY
I MUST NOT BULLY
I MUST NOT BULLY
UNO
ILLINGWORTH

WITH APOLOGIES TO JOHN RALPH MERTON

PROBLEM PICTURE

"Problem Picture" by Illingworth (1958): This image is based bizarrely on a portrait of the Countess of Dalkeith by John Ralph Merton. This time Nasser is holding a copy of *How to Win Friends and Influence People* by Dale Carnegie, a popular self-help book first published in 1936. In July 1956, Egypt's leader Nasser announced the nationalization of the Suez Canal, much to the chagrin of Britain and France who secretly sent troops to take it back. The US made its allies back off and accept the UN proposal to create a peace-keeping force for the canal. It was a humiliation that eventually led to the resignation of Foreign Secretary Anthony Eden.

OPPOSITE: "I Must not Bully" by Illingworth (1956): Watched by Nasser, Britain, Israel, and France are punished by the UN for trying to bully the Egyptians over the Suez Canal, while behind teacher's back Khrushchev is busy beating up Hungary (which had risen up against the USSR).

'THIS HURTS ME MORE THAN IT HURTS YOU!'

Ed Valtman '62
The Hartford Times

Nikita Khrushchev is about to extract missiles from Fidel Castro's mouth which are drawn in as teeth in this cartoon by Ed Valtman. In 1962, the US discovered that the Soviet Union was installing nuclear missiles on nearby Cuba. President John F. Kennedy announced he was blockading the island to prevent delivery of any more weapons. President Khrushchev immediately threatened war if Russian ships were stopped by the US, but finally agreed to remove the missiles. The rest of the world breathed a huge sigh of relief. Many thought the world was about to end in nuclear war.

"They Won't Get Us to the Conference Table… Will They?" by Pat Oliphant (1966): Ho Chi Minh, Vietcong leader, holds a dead man in his arms. Presumably, he was in that position as a direct result of Ho Chi Minh's refusal to discuss peace with America. This cartoon won the 1967 Pulitzer Prize.

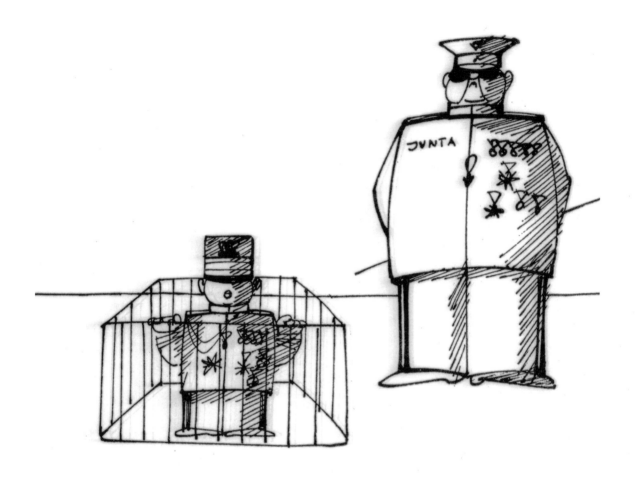

KONSTANTIN DER KLEINE

"Little Constantine" (1967): A German cartoon shows Greek king Constantine II under the control of the generals as a boy. When he grew up, the king organized a counter-coup against the generals who had taken over the country, but it went wrong and he had to flee Greece. He went into exile, never to return.

After the British had helped to set up the Federation of Malaysia in 1963, President Sukarno of Indonesia boasted that he would crush the fledgling state by the time the cock crowed at dawn on January 1, 1965. He tried to do so by sending in his troops. This cartoon was rush-released to newspapers for publication by a crowing Malaysian government on 31 December 1964: Sukarno had failed to conquer them. In 1967 Sukarno was put under house arrest by his own army. He died of kidney failure in 1970.

'Isn't it time you went home, Mum?'

"Isn't It Time You Went Home, Mum?" by Franklin (1968): Alexander Dubcek sits up in bed with a young lady called "Czech Freedom"—in between the couple sits the rather forbidding figure of Soviet leader Leonid Brezhnev. This cartoon is about the Prague Spring, when Czech leader Dubcek sought to liberalize life in his country. Reformer Dubcek wanted "a new model of socialism" and his country had four months of freedom in 1968 before 500,000 Warsaw Pact troops invaded and the Prague Spring turned to deepest winter. Dubcek was arrested and sent to Moscow.

OPPOSITE: "General Pinochet" by David Levine (1973): Full-length portrait of Chilean general Augusto Pinochet wearing a bloody apron over his military uniform. Pinochet became president of Chile after the emergency that ended the tenure of the democratically elected socialist president Salvador Allende. He was dictator of Chile from 1973 to 1990: in the aftermath of the CIA-backed coup which brought him to power, over 2,000 Chilean people were murdered, up to 80,000 were interned, and as many as 30,000 were tortured.

Modern Despots, Demagogues, and Control Freaks

"We've held a General Election and we Generals all voted against him"

"We've held a General Election and We Generals All Voted Against Him" by Keith Waite (1973): The Argentinean generals attend Allende's funeral in full force, with big dark glasses and epaulettes like aircraft landing strips. The official version of Allende's death was that he committed suicide with an AK-47 assault rifle during the coup of 1973. But many people refused to accept the military junta's verdict because they believed he had been assassinated.

OPPOSITE: "Peron" by David Levine (1979): Portrait of Argentina's president and dictator Juan Peron, toothy smile belied by the oversized thuggish body and knuckle-dusters on his hands. Peron was president of Argentina three times and was married to the famous Eva (Evita) who died in 1952 aged 33. He facilitated rat runs for Nazi war criminals to come to Argentina after 1945 and stamped down on freedom of speech despite much-vaunted claims to represent the working man. In 1974 Peron was buried in La Chacarita Cemetery, Buenos Aires. In 1987, his tomb was defiled and the hands of his corpse stolen. Those responsible have never been found.

Modern Despots, Demagogues, and Control Freaks | 171

Kal Kallaugher, The Economist, 12.7.1980, The British Cartoon Archive, University of Kent, www.cartoons.ac.uk

"Robert Mugabe" by Kal (Kevin Kallaugher) (1980): Mugabe threatens to expel members of Zimbabwe's white diplomatic community. Mugabe's crimes include genocide against supporters of political opponent Joshua Nkomo (at least 20,000 were killed by the North Korea-trained Fifth Brigade), throwing 4,000 white farmers off their land, and bringing starvation to his previously fertile country, with inflation reaching a world-record 10^{25} per cent.

"Amin" by Ed Valtman (undated): Idi Amin, president of Uganda from 1971 to 1979, loved to award himself medals and titles. He called himself His Excellency President for Life, Field Marshal Al Hadji Doctor, The Uncrowned King of Scotland, Idi Amin VC DSO MC and Conqueror of the British Empire. He was also one of the 20th century's worst tyrants, responsible for perhaps 500,000 deaths by the time he was exiled to Saudi Arabia in 1979. Before that, he had welcomed terrorist plane hijackers to Entebbe airport, unjustly expelled Uganda's Asian population so he could take away their businesses, and used his secret police to conduct mass executions of political opponents. Valtman portrays a watchful, bloated figure with a tiny head. Amin died in 2003 in Jeddah, Saudi Arabia at the age of 78. His major accomplishments had been to ruin Uganda's economy and spread terror wherever he went.

Nicholas Garland, The Daily Telegraph, 17.10.82, The British Cartoon Archive, University of Kent, www.cartoons.ac.uk

"Jaruzelski" by Nick Garland (1982): General Wojciech Jaruzelski was the last communist leader of Poland and the man who sent the tanks in to crack down on Solidarity, the first free trade union in the Soviet Bloc, in 1981 after the imposition of martial law. Jaruzelski claimed his actions had saved Poland from invasion by Russia and, five years later, he was more popular in Poland than his erstwhile foe, Solidarity leader Lech Walesa. Jaruzelski presided over the death of communism in Poland after the fall of the Berlin Wall, so the jury is out on whether he truly belongs in the Dictators' Hall of Infamy.

"... believe me, I had nothing to do with the TWA explosion, I was ... excuse me a minute! Abdul! How many times must I tell you, don't test explosives when I'm on the phone."

"... believe me, I had nothing to do with the TWA explosion, I was... excuse me a minute! Abdul! How many times must I tell you, don't test explosives when I'm on the phone" by Griffin (1986): It looks as if Colonel Gaddafi of Libya has come up with a new way of dealing with nuisance phone callers, but this cartoon was drawn in the wake of an explosion aboard a TWA flight bound for Athens, which killed four people. A group calling itself the Ezzedine Kassam Unit of the Arab Revolutionary Cells claimed responsibility, and said it was acting in retaliation for US bombing raids against Libya the previous month.

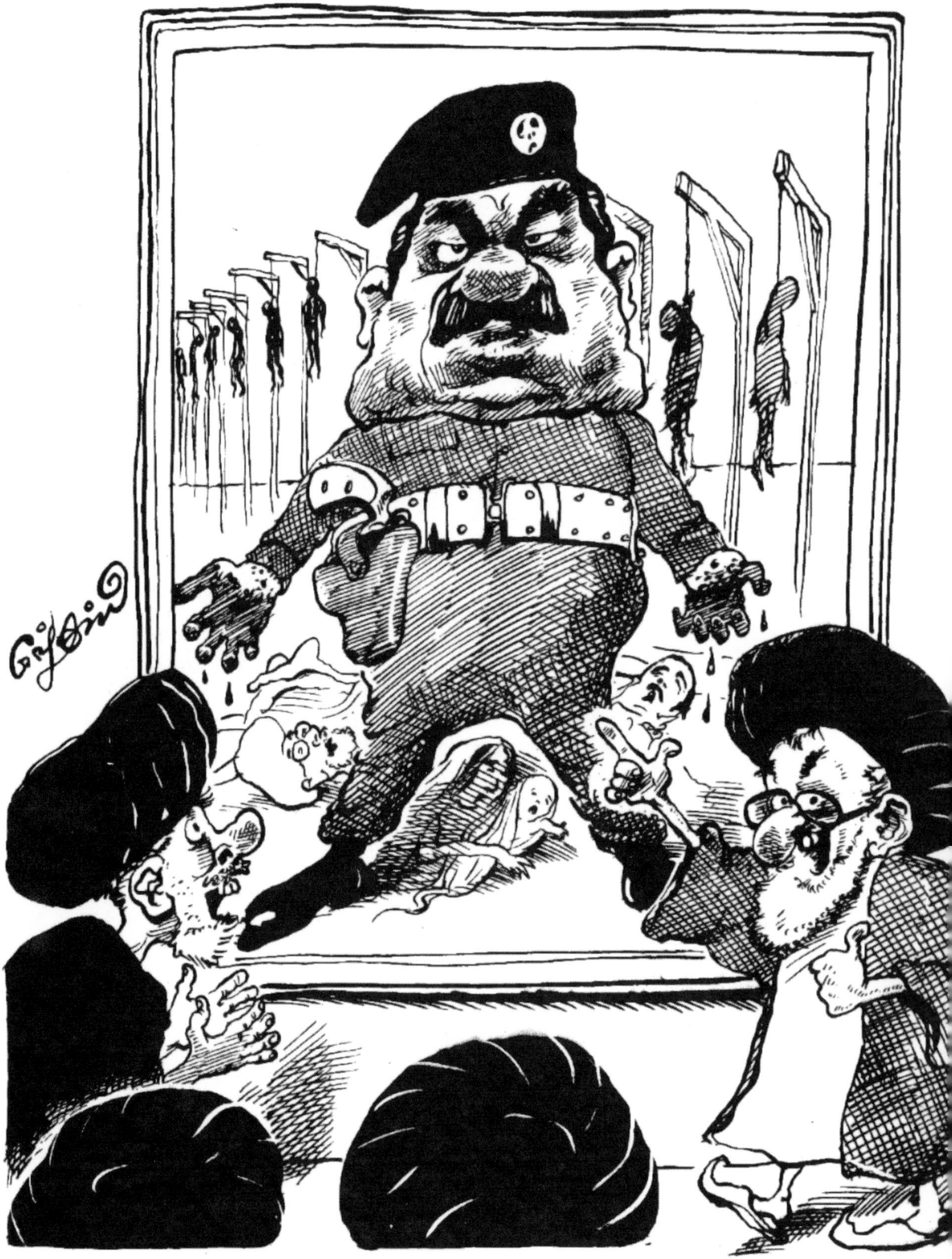

"Yup! He's Our Boy" by Griffin (1990): Iran's Ayatollah Khomeini knows who he'd choose between the murderous Saddam Hussein and George H. W. Bush. The Iran–Iraq War had just ended and diplomatic relations had been restored between Iran and Iraq.

"Yup! He's our boy."

OPPOSITE: "Thanks for letting me come here Marcos. I've brought the extra votes you asked for" by Griffin (1986): Baby Doc Duvalier was reluctant dictator of Haiti, a country which was more or less the family business—his father Papa Doc held a referendum on the eve of his death and the people endorsed his son by 2,391,916 votes to nil. No one should think for a second that there were any irregularities in voting procedures! Ferdinand Marcos was a hardline anti-democrat who called for self-sacrifice on the part of his people, while his wife, Imelda, embezzled funds to spend on her legendary shoe collection. The point is, both dictators were deposed within 18 days of one another in 1986 and each one was carried into exile aboard a US Air Force C-141… (not shown here).

LEFT: "General Zia" by Griffin (1988): This portrait appeared upon the death of Pakistan's chief of staff and president between 1978 and 1988. His record is not a good one. He crushed demands for democracy in the province of Sindh with helicopter gunships; he subjected opponents to public floggings; he tortured and persecuted his way to more and more power, sowing the seeds for the Taliban to take over Pakistan. "A" for effort, "F" for attitude and achievement!

OPPOSITE: "Pol Pot" by Nicholas Garland (1990): George H. W. Bush tries to keep Pol Pot and his killers from crossing the threshold, and that's because they shared a secret. It seems crazy now, but the US is alleged to have backed the murderous Pol Pot and his Khmer Rouge in a number of ways, including funding them with $85m between 1980 and 1986. The World Food Program is also alleged to have given food worth $12m to the Thai army to pass on to the Khmer Rouge.

"Thanks for letting me come here Marcos. I've brought the extra votes you asked for."

Nicholas Garland, *The Daily Telegraph*, 20.7.1990, The British Cartoon Archive, University of Kent, www.cartoons.ac.uk

"Pol Pot" by Chris Priestley (1998): Pol Pot took over Cambodia, a country much enfeebled by US bombing, in 1975, which he renamed Year Zero (possibly because he was a megalomaniac). He then set about ruining the lives of most Cambodians, punishing people who wore glasses for being "intellectuals", sending the 1.5 million city-dwellers of Phnom Penh to the countryside to work in the fields, and causing the deaths of 1.7m citizens from starvation, disease, and overwork. He was deposed in 1979, and died of a heart attack in his sleep deep in the Cambodian jungle in 1998.

Chris Priestley, *The Independent*, 17.4.1998, The British Cartoon Archive, University of Kent, www.cartoons.ac.uk

"Nicolae Ceausescu" by Griffin (1989): In Romania, Ceausescu ran the most rigidly Stalinist regime among the old Eastern Bloc satellite countries. His secret police, the *Securitate*, were feared throughout the land. He called himself the 'Genius of the Carpathians' and had a king-like scepter made to make him look more important. You might be able to forgive him his small vanities, but for the fact that he brutally destroyed the historic and beautiful core of his capital city Bucharest, replacing it with hideous dictator-style architecture intended to convey a sense of his personal power rather than anything more interesting. Things went badly wrong for him when he ordered his security forces to fire on demonstrators in the city of Timisoara in December 1989. It didn't have the intended effect, and soon he and his wife Elena were fleeing by helicopter, but they were tracked down and shot by firing squad, bringing the first successful revolution to occur in any communist country nicely to an end.

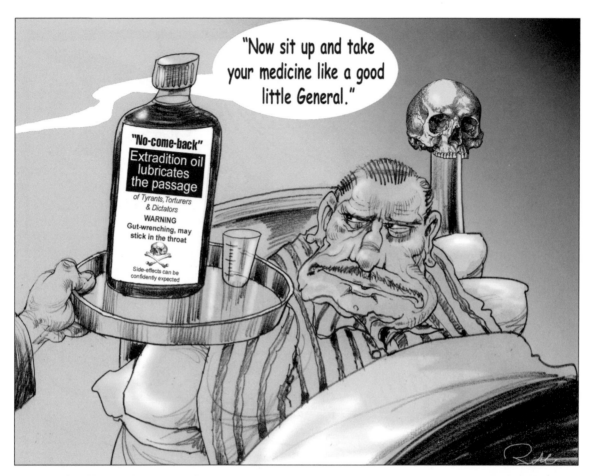

Bill McArthur, *The Glasgow Herald*, 26.11.1998, The British Cartoon Archive, University of Kent, www.cartoons.ac.uk

"No-come-back" by Bill McArthur (1998): As an old friend of Margaret Thatcher's, General Pinochet was invited to Britain in 1998 for medical treatment and, allegedly, to do some arms deals. Unfortunately, he was arrested in London, charged with human rights violations and held for 18 months. He returned to Chile, but died before he could appear in court on over 300 charges. The Rettig Report found conclusively that at least 2,279 persons were murdered in Chile by his government and that over 30,000 people were tortured. He also embezzled large amounts of money, much of this thought to have been raised from the illegal arms and drugs trades.

OPPOSITE: "I Can't Believe My Eyes" by Ed Valtman (1990): Lenin, Stalin, and the great god Marx look impotently down from communist paradise as Soviet leader Mikhail Gorbachev leads the funeral procession for communism. Everything they had fought for turned to dust after the fall of the Berlin Wall.

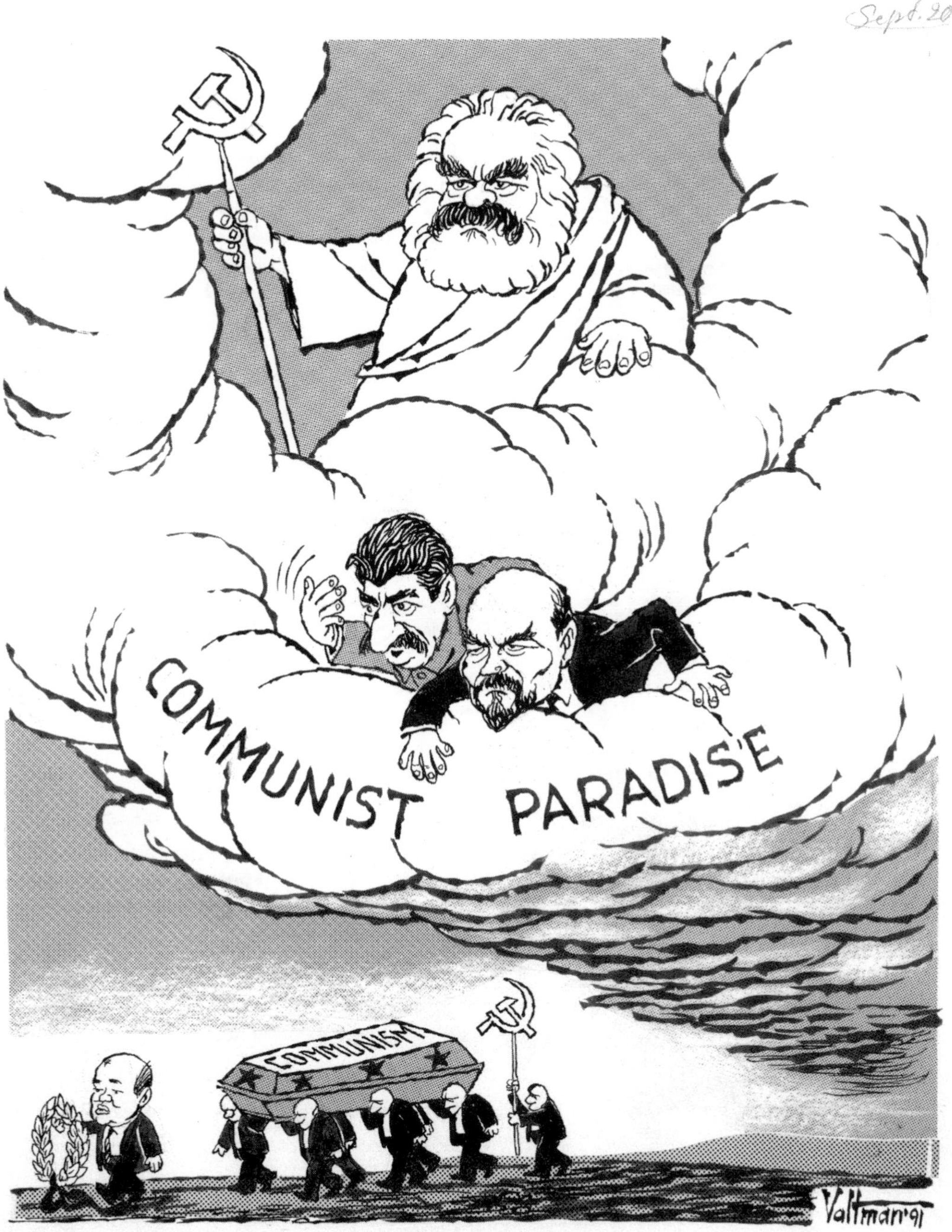
Sept. 20
COMMUNIST PARADISE
COMMUNISM
Valtman'91

'I CAN'T BELIEVE MY EYES!'

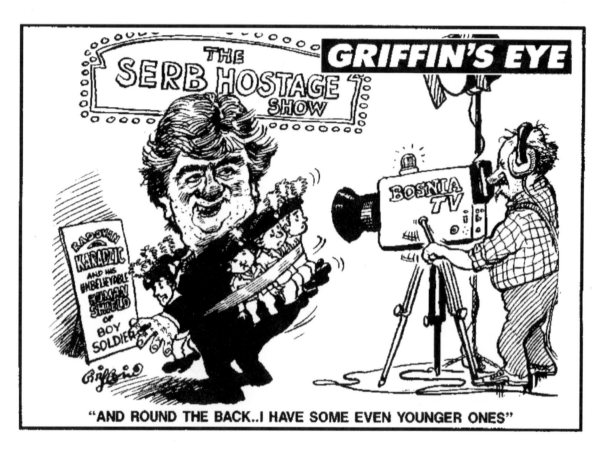

"AND ROUND THE BACK..I HAVE SOME EVEN YOUNGER ONES"

"And around the back… I have some even younger ones" by Griffin (1995): Radovan Karadzic and his Bosnian Serb militia seized 33 British hostages and attempted to use them as a human shield. Karadzic, a psychiatrist by trade, was accused of direct responsibility for the gravest atrocities in the Bosnian war, "the worst crimes committed in Europe since World War II." After being indicted by the International Criminal Tribunal, he was arrested in 2008 and, at time of writing, still awaits sentence.

Opposite: "Special Invitation" by Herb Block (1999): Hands drenched in blood, Slobodan Milosevic stands on the bodies of the victims of ethnic cleansing in the Balkans asking people if they want some more. In 1999, while president of Serbia, Milosevic was charged by the International Criminal Tribunal with war crimes, including genocide and crimes against humanity in connection with wars in Bosnia, Croatia, and Kosovo. At his five-year-long trial in The Hague, he conducted his own defence rather cleverly and the trial ended without a verdict. On March 11, 2006 he died of a heart attack.

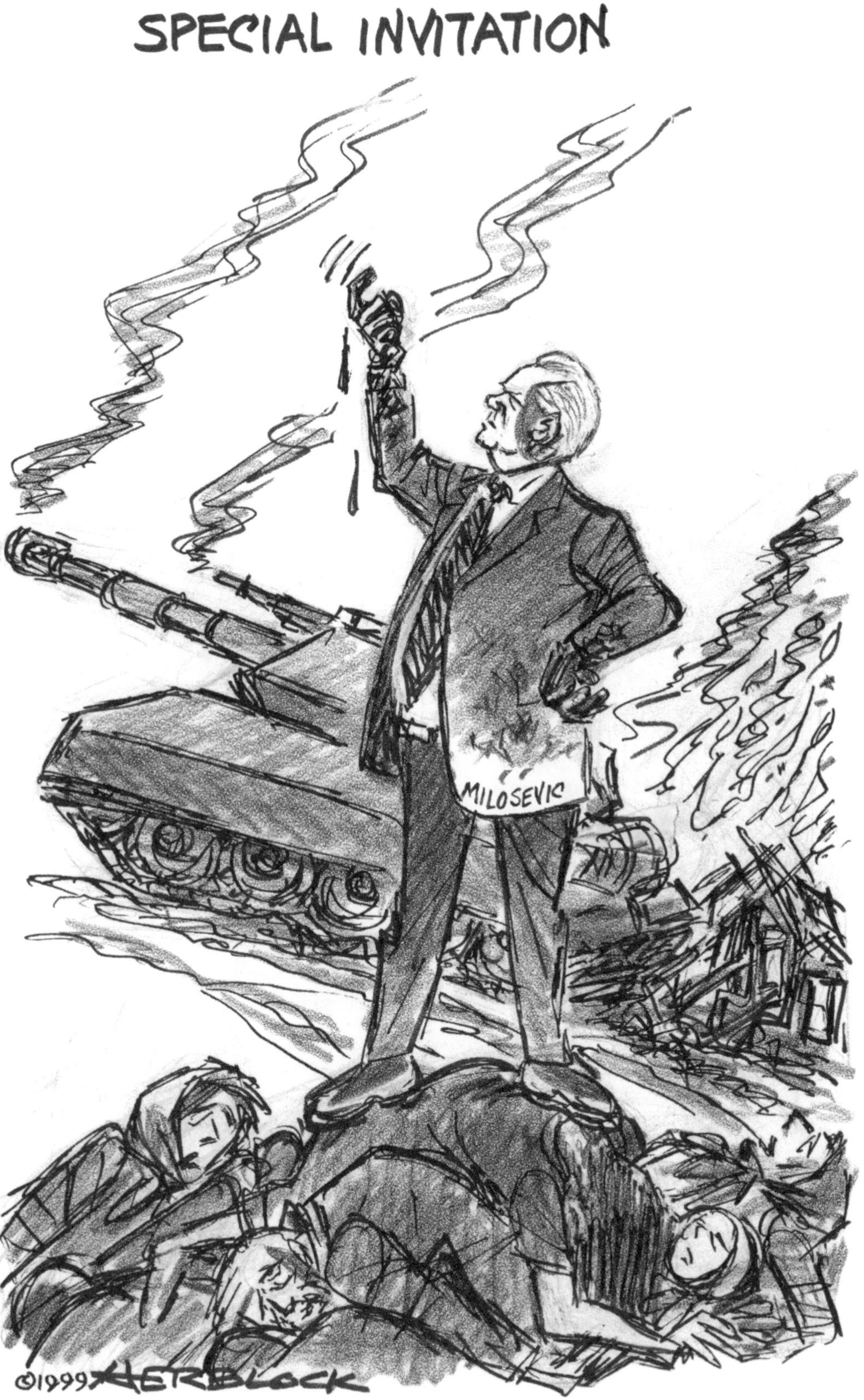
SPECIAL INVITATION
MILOSEVIC
©1999 HERBLOCK

Chris Priestley, *The Independent*, 20.5.1998, The British Cartoon Archive, University of Kent, www.cartoons.ac.uk

"Trust me, I'm a Dictator" by Chris Priestley (1998): President Suharto was absolute dictator of Indonesia, the world's largest Muslim country. When he took over from the deposed Sukarno in 1967, at least 500,000 Indonesians, mostly from East Java and northern Sumatra, were killed, but the figure could have been three or four times higher. Nobody was keeping score. When Suharto invaded East Timor, 230,000, a third of the population, died. The West sold him as many weapons as he wanted and they were used to repress his own people and deny them free speech. Suharto turned out to be one of the worst mass murderers of the 20th century. On top of that, he plundered between $15bn and $30bn from the people of Indonesia.

"A Bit More Practice on the pronunciation… all together now…
welcome… Slobodan Milosevic!" by Tom Johnston (1999):
"Slobba" rolls up in Hell and gets a warm welcome from those in
the Top Dictators hot tub: Stalin, Pol Pot, Mussolini, Hitler, and
the Emperor Nero… or is it Caligula? (See pages 16 and 17.)

'A BIT MORE PRACTICE ON THE PRONUNCIATION...ALL TOGETHER NOW...WELCOME SLOBODAN MILOSEVIC!'

Tom Johnston, *The Daily Mirror*, 31.3.1999, The British Cartoon Archive, University of Kent, www.cartoons.ac.uk

"Kim Il Sung" by Rod Coddington (1993): Kim Il Sung was ruler of North Korea from its foundation in 1948 until 1994 when he died. He was known as the Great Leader or the Eternal President, and he was a prolific builder of larger and larger statues to himself. Remarkably, even though he is dead, he is still officially president of the country, general secretary of the Workers Party, and chairman of the Party Central Military Commission. The Great Leader's regime was responsible for over one million deaths through concentration camps, forced labor and executions.

"Putin" by Bramhall (2014): Punk group Pussy Riot were attacked by Cossack militia men with whips and teargas at the Winter Olympics city of Sochi. They were singing "Putin Will Teach You to Love the Motherland" at the time. Two members of Pussy Riot had earlier been jailed for two years for performing a "punk prayer" in Moscow's main cathedral. When Putin came back for his third term, he realized he couldn't preach communism any more, so instead he clamped down on dissent, silencing anyone who did not obey him.

"Kim Jong Un" by Bramhall (2014): The North Koreans hacked Sony Pictures and Kim Jong Un demanded that *The Interview*, a $42m satire about his monstrous rule, should not be shown in US cinemas. Sony refused at first but then decided to accede and withdrew it. They still released it on video at Christmas. As grandson of Kim Il Sung, Kim Jong Un has a lot to live up to. In 2011, he compelled anyone sharing his name to change it. He is also alleged to have had his uncle machine-gunned to death. Meanwhile his wife still equips herself with handbags costing a year's annual salary for the average North Korean. As human rights violations continue unabated, Kim Jong Un proves again and again that he's a chip off the old blocks, father Kim Jong Il and grandad Kim Il Sung.

OPPOSITE: "One Day, Son, All This Will Be Yours" by Tony Husband (2015): It can't be much fun being the son of a dictator, watching as your father destroys your inheritance before your eyes. This cartoon sums up dictators. They always destroy far more than they create.

one day, son, all this will be yours

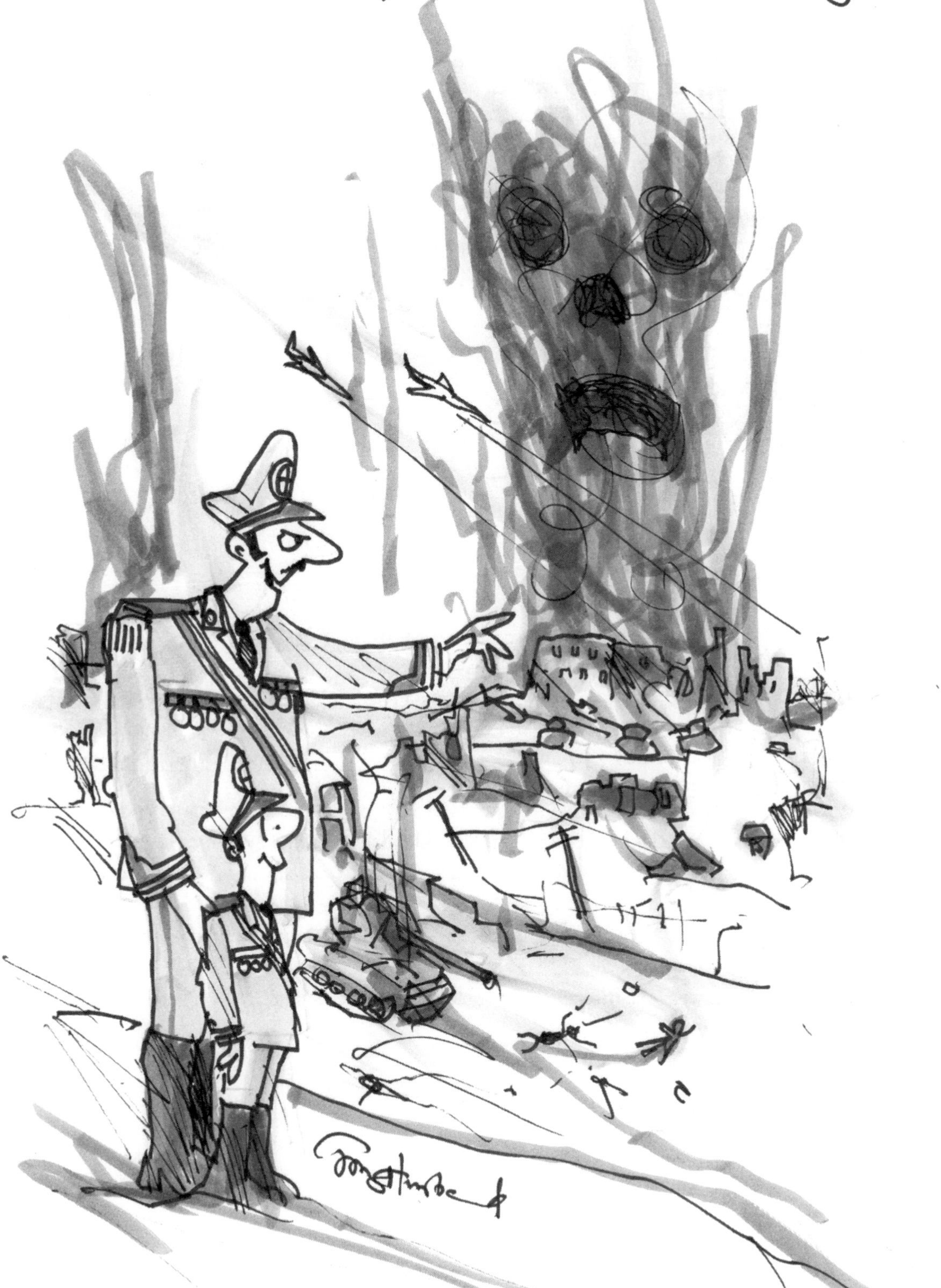

Picture Credits

We have made every effort to contact the copyright holders of the images used in this book. In a few cases we have been unable to do so, but we will be very happy to credit them in future editions.

US Library of Congress: 7 (Reproduced with the cooperation of The Arthur Szyk Society, Burlingame, CA), 8, 9, 14-15, 23 (t&b), 25, 28, 29 (t&b), 30, 35, 37, 39, 40-41, 49, 61, 66, 68, 69, 74, 75 (b), 80, 81 (t), 82, 86, 87 (By permission of the Marcus family), 88, 89, 98 (By permission of the Marcus family), 99, 117 (By permission of the Marcus family),120, 124, 130, 131, 132, 133 (t), 135, 136, 147, 148-149, 153, 160, 164, 165, 169 (© Matthew and Eve Levine), 171 (© Matthew and Eve Levine), 173, 183, 185,

Corbis: 10, 16, 17, 18, 20, 21, 24, 34, 38, 42, 62, 161, 167

Punch: 11, 13, 26-27, 36, 47, 55, 58, 63, 64, 65, 70-71, 79, 81 (b), 84, 85, 91, 95, 100, 104, 106, 107, 108, 116, 118, 119, 127, 137, 142-143, 144, 145, 150, 152, 159, 162, 163,

Mirrorpix: 12, 52-53, 67, 83, 92-93, 140-141, 151, 155, 156-157, 168, 170, 175, 176-177, 178, 179, 181, 184,

Topfoto: 22 (t), 31, 32-33, 44, 46, 48, 51, 59, 72, 76-77, 78, 94, 102, 113 (b), 114, 115, 122, 128, 154, 166,

Getty: 19, 43, 54, 101 (b), 113 (t), 188, 189, 190

Mary Evans: 45, 50, 125

British Cartoon Archive, University of Kent: 56, 57 (t) (Kem image courtesy of Richard and Alexander Marengo), 57 (b), 60, 96, 97, 103, 110, 111, 146, 158, 172, 174 (thanks to Nicholas Garland), 179 (thanks to Nicholas Garland), 180 (thanks to Chris Priestley), 182 (thanks to Bill McArthur), 186 (credit needed), 187 (credit needed)

Wikimedia: 73, 75 (t), 101 (t), 105 (t), 105 (b), 109, 112, 123, 133 (b), 138, 139

Bridgeman: 126

RIA Novosti: 143

State Historical Society of Missouri: 90, 121

The University of Minnesota: 129

Tony Husband: 191